SCIENTOLOGY
– More Than A Cult?
From Crusade To Rip-Off.
The Principles Unveiled.

SCIENTOLOGY

More Than A Cult?

From Crusade To Rip-Off.

.

.   .

The Principles Unveiled.

EDITION SCIENTERRA

"That the Freedom of the Press
is one of the great Bulwarks of Liberty
and can never be restrained
but by dispotic Governements."

The Bill of Rights,
Art. 11,
28th of June, 1776.

SCIENTOLOGY – More Than A Cult?
Subtitles: From Crusade To Rip-Off + The Principles Unveiled

For information or orders please address VAP Delivery Service, Post Box 1180, D-4994 Preussisch Oldendorf – Germany.

ISBN 3-922367-26-7, Verkehrs-Nr. 16645 (BAG)
First printing 1991
Printed in Germany

Table of contents

Publisher's Foreword

Dear Reader,

let us be honest: who nowadays would read a classical novel of 600 or more pages? Who could still manage to enjoy Goethe's Faust, for example, late in the evening after a hard day's work? In order to hold their place against the flood of manuals on gardening, cooking and car repairing, standard classical works are already being abbreviated to an "acceptable" extent. This facilitates the reader's entry into a new area; and perhaps it leads on to his reading the original text. Even the Bible has suffered this fate – one could only wish that such attempts fully took into account its religious and philosophical aspects. In this context it does not seem inappropriate that VAP is issuing, in a similar manner, a work which started as a bestseller and has continued to sell for over forty years now, totalling 15 million copies worldwide: L.Ron Hubbard's book "Dianetics". In the present work, "Dianetics" is being represented with full respect for its authenticity; the philosophical and technical developments over the last 40 years are dealt with; the various ways of applying the ideas and procedures of scientology are pointed out. The original manuscript behind this book (it became stranded at the publisher's like a message in a bottle) has been written by a high-ranking insider. His profound knowledge and many years of experience with the subject of dianetics and scientology allowed him to produce a reliable synopsis of Hubbard's writings. After a critical treatment on the part of the publisher, a homogenous and understandable book could be put together. Its first two parts are herewith presented to the reader. In doing this, the publisher aims to rid a hot subject of its taboos and contribute to the information available to the broad public.

PART ONE:

From Crusade to Rip-Off.

"The motto of this universe
is 'we must have a game'.
The game is the thing.
The wins and losses are not the thing.
One loses every time one wins,
for he then has no game."
(L.Ron Hubbard, "Creation of Human Ability".)

Preface

To start off with an anecdote: when I – a young student at the scientology organisation at St.Hill, England, – took my first training courses in the mid-seventies, I was all curiosity and enthusiasm. Yet already in the first week of my being there I had a rather sobering experience, the significance of which didn't dawn on me till many years later.

Right outside the courseroom area, on the lawn, there were some benches. They served – in summer – as an "open air waiting room" for the public who took services in the organisation. Sitting on one of these benches I met an old man. He was crying. When I asked him what the matter was, he answered: "Scientology is a marvellous thing if it weren't for the people who run it."

This simple statement contains – in a nutshell – the whole paradox of scientology. Its founder called it "an applied religious philosophy", but what you see from the outside is big business, scandals, extortion of money from people, governments banning it, the press tearing it up, and what not. On the one hand you have L.Ron Hubbard, a prolific writer and free thinker, and on the other hand a Church of Scientology which anxiously and jealously keeps Hubbard's teachings a secret and considers itself to have a monopoly on them. Here is a man who – in his "Code of a Scientologist" – gives all scientologists the right *"to keep Scientologists, the Public and the Press accurately informed concerning Scientology (. . .)"*, and there you have an apparatus which condemns and prosecutes anyone who does so [1].

Much has been said about the Church of Scientology (abbreviated to "CofS" from here on) in the media, none of it was good. Much has been said about L.Ron Hubbard, none of it complimentary. I am not going to repeat it. It can be read elsewhere. Yet in order to show how a basically good thing became distorted and perverted partly by its founder and partly by the apparatus he built to promote it, I will have to dedicate Part One of this book to the development of scientology, its founder and the CofS. Mainly, though, I am going to talk about the thing itself, about the intention and the crusade of Hubbard, about scientology philosophy and its application. This is the concern and the purpose of this book. What is this thing called scientology? What makes people at first rave about it and later condemn it, waste their lives and finances for it, makes them put the blame for their spiritual happiness and failure on it? Is it useful or isn't it? Does it help or does it destroy? – These questions I will try to suggest answers to.

When I assert that scientology is a "basically good thing", I am speaking from my own background of a good ten thousand hours spent doing therapy work with its methods. The time after 1983 plays a greater role regarding the therapy concepts I developed than the time before. This is because in 1983 the fascist machinations inside the Church of Scientology had reached their peak; out of protest I resigned from my membership – along with thousands of others – and started my own practice. Over the years I succeeded in stripping off the mental narrowness the CofS cultivates in its members and approaching the core of the matter, both in theory and in practice. The teachings of Hubbard do offer many possibilities of helping people – be it with regard to their troubles and sorrows or their psychosomatic illnesses. *How* one uses this body of knowledge, is a different matter. Whether one uses it successfully or not, depends on how well one understands it. This is of course true for any body of knowledge. It may be that it gets turned into an ideology, developing all sorts of dogmas, and with a personality cult growing up around its founder, as happened with the CofS. And it must be partly the founder who is to blame and partly the people who follow him in their bigoted way. However, what counts in the end, are positive results.

Dianetics –
The Book That Sparked It Off

Scientology didn't get started off under this name. The initial
impetus for the movement occurred in 1950 under the name of
"dianetics" when Hubbard's first book appeared, "Dianetics,
Modern Science of Mental Health" (DMSMH for short, also
called Book One). **Dianetics** means – with a bit of an etymological somersault – "through the mind", taken from Greek
"dia", through, and "nous", mind. The term is meant to signify
that all troubles and ills man may suffer stem from mental dis-
orders and can be cured by looking at them "through the
mind". The book – more than 400 pages in the hardcover edition – was written within six weeks only, and that's what it
looks like. What the reason for the haste may have been, remains unclear – after all, Hubbard had been busy exploring
the human mind for a good two decades already. Why did he
hurry then? Was it because of the 86 000 dead at Hiroshima?
The 75 000 dead at Nagasaki? The increase of rocket speed and
accelerating rush towards space travel?

"Dianetics" presents a theory on the human mind which can
be applied in the form of a therapy called "auditing". As well,
it proposes that anyone who reads this book can turn himself
into an auditor and audit his family and friends or even become a professional. And it asserts strongly and unequivocally
that drugs, hypnosis, physical violence against patients and
electric shocks – all in the name of "therapy" – are strictly evil
and not needed at all in order to help one's fellow man.

Dianetics rests on the basis of the desire for optimum survival
inherent in each living thing. Man, as well as other thinking
and feeling beings, wants to feel well physically and to attain
the goals he has for himself, for his family and for his business
and public life. Anything stopping him he looks at as contrasurvival. When the opposition is so great that he breaks down
under the strain of fighting it, the resulting shock and pain is

recorded and leads – as time goes by – to sorrowfulness and psychosomatic illnesses.

To quote Hubbard: *"The dynamic principle of existence – SURVIVE! (. . .) The reward for survival activity is pleasure. (. . .) The ultimate penalty of destructive activity is death or complete nonsurvival, and is pain. (. . .) Happiness is the overcoming of not unknown obstacle towards a known goal and, transiently, the contemplation of indulgence in pleasure."* ("The Fundamental Axioms of Dianetics", to be found in "Dianetics" or in [1].)

(All words appearing in **bold** print can be found in the "Scientology Technical Dictionary" [2].)

DIANETIC THERAPY

Auditing is Hubbard's name for his brand of therapy. Taken from Latin audire, to listen, it simply means "listening". Hubbard didn't like to use the word therapy as it is fraught with connotations from the medical and psychiatric field which Hubbard didn't wish to be mixed up with. His intention was not primarily to "repair" the handicapped but "to make the able more able".

In an auditing session the auditor asks his client about times of trouble in his life and helps him to discharge upsetting memories in such a way that they can be looked at with ease. What's being taken away is not the actual memory of the incident but the charge accumulated regarding it. **Charge** is a mental energy phenomenon felt by anyone who experiences something unpleasant, dangerous or lethal, something – in a word – which goes against his idea of optimum survival concerning any aspect of his life (not only the mere physical one of food and shelter). Charge occurs at the moment a serious countereffort to one's survival efforts is received. It is also felt at the moment of such an incident being restimulated through the association of some element of the present environment with some element in the past incident. A typical example: little

Johnny falls off his bike and hurts his leg, with the consequence that he doesn't like to ride his bike any more and later on breaks out in tears at the sight of his and maybe even other bikes. When the incident is of considerable severity, such **restimulation** is likely to occur years and even decades later, given that the pertinent triggers are prevalent in the person's surroundings.

Charge is manifested by misemotions such as anger, fear, grief, apathy or death wishes. In auditing, misemotions and psychosomatic ills are traced down to their basic incident, i.e. the first time the contrasurvival effort (illness, accident, violence, prenatal stress) occurred. This incident is called an **engram**. As the example above demonstrates, it is almost unavoidable that one reacts to engrams once they are restimulated. All engrams taken together therefore form a "reactive data bank", or simply **bank**.

The trouble vanishes as soon as the client has re-experienced in his session those parts of the original incident which – up to this point – were hidden under a layer of unconsciousness. **Unconsciousness** plays the crucial role in keeping an engram in place. As long as any part of an engram is not fully viewed it can be restimulated, i.e. reactivated by the environment. Some engrams contain only split seconds of unconsciousness, others hours and days of it. Any amount of unconsciusness is sufficient to keep an engram intact and restimulatable. Its like a timebomb ticking away forever and occasionally blowing up, yet never losing its potential to blow up again.

"PRE-CLEAR" AND "CLEAR"

The client – in the jargon of dianetics – is called a **preclear** or **pc**. This means that he isn't clear – or a **Clear** – yet. He isn't clear because he still has a **case**. His case consists of the amount of charge which happens to be in restimulation; in other words, all the active engrams which pour their charge over the person add up to his case.

Making a person "go clear" is the sole purpose of auditing; it is the basis of the auditor's and the pc's co-operation; it is their common endeavour. The state of Clear is attained when all engrams have been erased. The person is then free of all potentially restimulatable material and can live and act without interference from unwanted thoughts, emotions, physical sensations or pains. He is not **aberrated** any longer. This result can be achieved and has been achieved. It does take work, though, in some cases a few hundred hours. The result is highly appreciated by those who have attained it.

The concept of Clear implies that the abilities of a being are not brought about by fortunate social structures or a happy childhood, but by his amount of reactivity alone. "Reactive behaviour" triggered by a restimulation is synonymous with irrational, insane, not solution-oriented behaviour. The less reactivity someone has, the more he will be able to correctly assess his abilities, take an opportunity and apply them successfully.

These thoughts are by no means new; elsewhere they come under the heading of "karma", the idea that anything happening to someone at all is to a large extent his own fault. If he has done something bad and walks around with a bad conscience, he is withdrawn and doesn't pay the neccessary attention to his environment. He is liable to have an accident quite easily. When this incident is recorded as an engram, reactivity will arise from it later. But before there was reactivity there was one's own responsibility – and that precisely is karma, as the Buddhists call it.

Hubbard's Mission

L. Ron Hubbard's life background as stated by him and promoted by the CofS has been widely debated and doubted. It is the subject of a good half-dozen books which are out to leave not a single good spot on the man's character. Whatever: He was born in 1911 in Nebraska, USA, and travelled a fair bit in his youth due to international family ties. At the age of twenty he started to support himself by writing. Allegedly he participated in the first nuclear physics course in the US. It seems certain that he learnt to fly airplanes, achieved his captain's license for all oceans and joined the navy as an officer during the war. Eye witnesses narrate that he was severely hurt in a wreck diving accident and barely came through. His companion died in the explosion. Hubbard, who had already done research into the mind before the war already, applied his knowledge to himself and – quite miraculously – got himself going again. (He claims to have been trained in psychoanalysis, by the way.) In 1948 he summarized his findings in a then unpublished manuscript called "The Original Thesis" which contains the philosophical and technical approaches of dianetics in rudimentary form. (It was published in 1951 after his success with "Dianetics".)

Having had published some hundreds of adventure and science fiction stories, Hubbard was – by the time he started dianetics – financially all set up "to get the show on the road" (one of his favourite terms). He didn't have to "invent a religion" in order to make money. He was – as we will see – honestly concerned with the welfare and the spiritual enhancement of man. However, his intentions are one thing; the way they came across and were interpreted by others, are a different thing altogether.

DMSMH (Dianetics, Modern Science of Mental Health), as mentioned earlier, was written within six weeks only. To Hubbard, his message was an urgent issue; it had to be brought out fast, fast, fast. This sense of urgency, and some other aspects of DMSMH – verbosity, pioneer spiritedness and a sloppy rendition of grand thoughts – sets the stage for the thirty years of research which were to follow (from 1948, to be exact, when Hubbard's first manuscripts were circulated, till 1978). Hubbard kept being verbose, pioneer spirited and sloppy, and he kept urging, urging, urging himself, the staff, the public; pushing them up and forward to attain the humanly unattainable, to superhuman feats of labour, suffering and success.

The subject of "the tech" (i.e. auditing techniques) grew and grew. "Breakthroughs" were proudly announced by Hubbard, only to be discarded soon – in the light of his latest research – and to be followed by new breakthroughs. Because of this thirty-year turmoil the tech was never rounded up, finalized and brought into a handy form. Hubbard exited from the stage in 1978, leaving behind a vast amount of written and taped materials: eight books written within the ten years after 1950; an unending avalanche of technical bulletins, originally issued as loose leaves and, when bound, totalling a good five thousand pages (the twelve "Tech Volumes"); some six thousand taped lectures given within twenty years; about two thousand policy letters acting as organizational instructions to the CofS and filling ten volumes of 450 pages each (the "Management Volumes").

The man kept himself busy finding ever-increasing challenges, no doubt. His heritage is twofold: first, an unwieldy pile of brilliant thoughts and definitions which keep changing from one research phase to the next and therefore appear incoherent and contradictory. They are held together by vast yet unstated concepts only detectable when one manages to read between the lines. The subject of scientology doesn't open itself easily for inspection. Read DMSMH or some other book, read any technical instruction, listen to any tape: they are all built around the same idea; but what exactly is it? – The second part of his heritage: a church which to all the world seems a bunch of supersecretive and possibly criminal lunatics. What, precisely, is this "Church"?

Hubbard saw his mission in "clearing the planet"; his tool was the Church of Scientology. "Clearing the planet" meant as much as freeing it from those clandestine suppressive powers which have shaped the history of Earth and which Hubbard recognizes as coming out of the unconscious part of man's mind. The background and implications of Hubbard's mission will become apparent as we go along in this introduction. To put it simply: he wanted to win the race against the atom bomb. He wanted to keep mankind from committing planetary suicide by developing weapons beyond their own control. A poignant quotation dating from 1952 sums it up: *"My purpose is to bring a barbarism out of the mud it thinks conceived it and to form, here on Earth, a civilization based on human understanding, not violence. That's a big purpose. A broad field. A starhigh goal. But I think it's your purpose, too."* [1]

The Beginning of Scientology

DMSMH was a smash success immediately after it came out. One shouldn't forget that in the fifties, in the field of mental care, there was nothing officially accepted but psychiatry and psychoanalysis. The psychological therapies for individuals and groups which have sprung up in the last four decades were not around then. There was no yoga, no meditation, no esoterics, no New Age movement. This is why Hubbard's book went off like a bomb. It formed a real alternative to the psychoterror of a psychiatry torturing its victims with drugs, electric schocks and brain amputations. When you were in trouble, back then, and when your doctor came to the end of his art, the psychiatrist was next in line. Psychoanalysis was too costly for most people, electric shocks however were paid for by your health insurance. Now, with "Dianetics", there was a chance to help oneself and one's fellow man! Small wonder that Hubbard's book was widely read and applied. People bought it, read it and audited each other. Soon a need for coordination and systematic instruction arose. The Hubbard Dianetic Research Foundation was formed in Elizabeth, New Jersey. Branches were established in Los Angeles, New York, Chikago and Honolulu, the main centers being Elizabeth and Los Angeles.

After a grand start, the Foundation soon (1951) got into financial trouble due to lack of predictable results. Hubbard himself could audit, but nobody else could. An early follower of his purportedly helped out but in fact crashed the place totally and bought Hubbard's rights to his own brainchild, i.e. the publishing rights and copyrights on all the Foundation's publications, including "Dianetics – Modern Science of Mental Health". Hubbard was left standing emptyhanded.

In order to continue his work he started the "Hubbard College" and used the name "scientology" instead of dianetics. In late 1954 – after some legal battles – the dianetic copyrights and publishing rights were returned to Hubbard. By that time, however, the word scientology had become so widely promoted already that Hubbard stuck with it from there on out. Since then, the significance of the word "dianetics" is reduced to a particular auditing technique [4].

The term "scientology" is taken – by yet another etymological somersault – from Latin "scire", to know, and from the generally used Greek suffix "-ology", science of. So it's the science of how to know. Know what? Answers to the problems of life, of one's existence, of where one comes from before birth and where one goes to after death. One can see that Hubbard had gone a few steps beyond the simple therapeutic concept of DMSMH. His target now, with scientology, was to enable the individual to self-determinedly establish who he was, where he came from, why he was here, etc. He wanted people to find the truth within themselves instead of them following another's truth. Scientology, in Hubbard's words, is *"a religious philosophy in its highest meaning as it brings man to total freedom and truth."* [2]

Practically speaking, scientology is a set of methods which aids the individual to look at and have realizations about his existence. It does not provide any ready-made anwers to the student or preclear. It teaches mental mechanisms, how they can be a trap in life and how they can be used in auditing to get out of the trap. Auditing is the method to explore and gain insight in one's personal universe, one's private world.

The aim of dianetics was *"a healthy, happy, high IQ human being"*, that of scientology *"to increase spiritual freedom, intelligence, ability, and to produce immortality"*. (Both quotes in [2].) Naturally, immortality as such cannot be "produced" as one has it anyway. What can be produced, however, is the recognition of it.

A New View of Man

The years between 1950 and 1954 brought some considerable advances – the E-meter (electropsychometer), the knowledge of past lives and the "whole track" – which go far beyond the views commonly held by the natural sciences of the west.

THE WHOLE TRACK

DMSMH had stunned the world – the medical world in particular – with the proposition that prenatal life was sentient; that there was a thinking and feeling being inside the embryonic body. Amongst auditors this never was a point of discussion as most preclears had no difficulty contacting prenatal incidents and alleviating their psychosomatic problems after "running them out" (auditor jargon). However, when Hubbard discovered in 1951 that some seemingly unresolvable cases were getting swift results as soon as they contacted past life incidents, a storm of arguments for and against it broke loose in the auditor community. Hubbard thought it neccessary to quite strongly address his auditors regarding this matter: *" The auditor who insists on auditing the current lifetime only, when he has the whole track technique available, is wasting time and effort and is, in fact, swindling his preclear."* [5]

When the issue of past lives was investigated further it was found not to be limited only to a few hundred years back but to extend over a vast stretch of time which appeared to be in the magnitude of sixty trillion years. Later research showed it was in excess of four quadrillion years of recallable time. This is what Hubbard called the **whole track**.

Naturally, such time spans go back to periods before there were bodies or even the physical universe itself. Yet even before there was physical matter, energy, space or time there was the spirit, i.e. you and me. What exactly this means is covered in the next sections.

THE E-METER

1952, in his book "History of Man", Hubbard announces the tool which made the discovery of past lives possible: the E-meter. Hubbard had tried electro-encephalographs and police lie-detectors, but they hadn't satisfied him. The E-meter did the job. *"It compares (. . .) to existing devices as the electronic microscope compares to looking through a quartz stone."* [5]

The E-meter is – in electronic terms – no magic mystery box but a simple Wheatstone bridge which measures the resistence of the body as influenced by the electric field around it. It does not react to the amount of sweat on the hands of the pre-clear as some seem to think. When the pc contacts a charged area on his timetrack (restimulation), the electric field around his body is affected and causes a reaction (a "read") on the E-meter's needle. The auditor, by asking the pc to go deeper into reading areas, will get straighter and faster to the basic incident than by observation of the pc's skin colour, eye brightness, emotional tone and degree of introvertedness alone – the auditing style of DMSMH. With the E-meter, the auditor is able to react to signals from the pc so subtle that they aren't perceptible to his eye; the needle, though, tells the tale. The validity of needle reads is confirmed by the pc changing to the better, i.e. realizing something about the connectedness between past incidents and his present condition, brightening up and recovering physically and emotionally.

MAN, SOUL OR "THETAN" ?

Once it was established that man is more than a combination of his body and his social security card, there was a need to find the right term for the phenomenon. "Man" was no good as it referred too much to the physical aspect. "Soul" didn't serve as in the Christian tradition man "had" a soul; it wasn't customary to say that man *was* a soul or to wonder who and where the owner of the soul was. What to do?

A year earlier, in 1951, Hubbard had given a lot of thought to the philosophical foundations of dianetics. The result of his efforts were "The Axioms of Dianetics", numbering 194. He proposed a theory which – quite in opposition to physics – said that the source of life is comparable to pure thought, that all physical or psychic phenomena are derived from thought, that life derives from thought and not matter. This "life force" he termed **theta**, simply because the "th" in the word "thought" has its counterpart in the Greek letter "th", pronounced "theta".

He comes to the simple statement: *"A life organism is composed of matter and energy in space and time, animated by theta"* (Dn Axiom 11; [1]). This sentence is the cornerstone of Hubbard's philosophical edifice which concerns the interaction between **matter, energy, space and time (mest)** and theta. All struggles of man in his attempt to survive are interpreted with reference to it. (His book, "Science of Survival", written 1951, is fully devoted to this theme [16].)

Going back to "History of Man" and the problem of how to call "it" that has existed through the millenia and is neither man nor soul and maybe both together: Hubbard's solution was to call it "theta being" or simply **thetan**. To give an example: the preclear William Thompson (51 years old, engineer, married, two children, 178 cm tall, 81 kg weight) receives an auditing session. When he recalls an incident of falling off his bicycle at the age of five, he is referring to the same William Thompson he is now, although then (age 5) his physical and social description was entirely different. When he recalls in some other session how he was hanged by the neck for stealing horses in the year 1535, he is still referring to the same person he is now, with the difference that the body he owned then doesn't exist any more and that then he wasn't called William Thompson but Pepe Gonzalez and it all happened during the Mexican conquista. But it's his incident, it happened on his timetrack. He knows it to be so. This person, this spiritual entity of perennial duration which doesn't live or die but takes bodies (which live and die) in order to play his games and fulfill what he made his mind up to do, is called "thetan".

OUTSIDE THE BODY

As they kept running into past deaths and past lifetimes in their sessions, auditors began to understand the thetan as a wanderer from one body to the next. It became undeniably apparent that some people would leave their body right at the moment of death whereas others would hang around the dead body for a while -sometimes for a long while even. It as well became apparent that people would take new bodies any time between conception and birth, sometimes months after birth. Cases have been known where a person would leave an adult body after an accident and give it up for dead, with another one picking up this very body to make it his home. All sorts of variations on this theme were obviously possible. Proof of the matter was: does running this incident resolve the problem? If so, it must be true. The sheer number of occurrences itself made it hard to doubt the matter.

The phenomenon of being outside the body was observed even during sessions and given the term "going **exterior**". A preclear would suddenly have perceptions from a point exterior to the body, see the body from above, be outside in the street and see what was happening, etc. This triggered a lot of research. Hubbard developed a number of processes to cultivate this ability. They were released 1954 in the book "Creation of Human Ability". Someone who managed to stay and act stably outside the body was deemed an **Operating Thetan** or **OT**. "Operate" means as much as "act". An OT is someone who acts as a *thetan*, not as a body [2].

The feat of going exterior is of course not restricted to scientology but has been experienced and observed in all spiritual disciplines of the past as well as of the present. Quite a number of people can do it naturally. The ability to do so varies considerably from person to person. Some just feel bigger than their body – as if they were the peach and the body the kernel. Depending on the emotional state of the person the volume of space the person takes in, will vary. It may be of remarkable size. Others actually manage to completely "get out" of the body and "walk around" – to be fair, one has to admit that this is a peak experience which not many have had. Usually it does not last longer than a few seconds or minutes. At this time there is no method in scientology whereby one could reliably turn this into a stable ability, although, regrettably, the promise of achieving such a state has been used as a powerful selling point within the movement.

WHO MAKES THOSE PICTURES?

Running out the pc's past life incidents, astounding as it may seem, is an easy matter for the auditor to handle. All he has to do is go earlier and earlier with the pc, and eventually the basic incident (e.g. getting hanged) will become available to be run. The pc can recall anything on the timetrack, no matter how deep down, as long as there is charge on the incident. Once the charge is removed he can recall the incident again (out of session) whenever he is interested to do so.

Things turn a trifle more difficult for the auditor when the pc takes his pictures from somebody else's timetrack. To give one example of many: Mrs.Dimple spends the night in a room where someone was stabbed to death years before, semi-consciously perceives the pictures that person made and has a nightmare. As her perceptions weren't made in a calm and collected frame of mind but in a state of attenuated consciousness and terror, Mrs.Dimple got tied up with these pictures without her knowing or wanting to do so. And so she keeps having the occasional nightmare whenever those pictures get restimulated. Or she finds herself – sitting at her desk in the office – having daydreams of bloody daggers and black-hooded villains.

This issue of "borrowed pictures" may sound even more surprising (except to those who have nightmares) than the issue of having lived before this life, but – looking at it in strictly technical terms – it isn't. A picture is nothing but **mental energy** condensed to **mental matter**. It is "solidified" or "frozen" attention. It exists in the person's **mental space** and contains a certain stretch of **mental time**. Pictures, therefore, are **mental mest** (matter + energy + space + time) – different from physical mest only by degrees: physical mest is more compressed than mental mest.

Some **mental image pictures** are made up the moment one wishes to see them and unmade the moment one doesn't need them any longer. This is true for pleasure moments or creative images of the things one sets out to construct, paint or compose. These are easy to control. Other pictures, though, seem to have a life of their own. They come at the wrong moment, one doesn't quite know where from, and distract and irritate one. These pictures are obviously less easily controllable. Their source are engrams. They are the information stored in engrams, i.e. in moments of such physical or mental duress that the person (thetan) was overwhelmed and succumbed and went unconscious. And what did he do just before going unconscious? He fought against the contrasurvival inflow by pushing energy against it, physical energy (his muscle power) and mental energy (his will power.)

This mental energy – condensed and solidified – is called a **ridge**. The term is to be understood as an analogy to its physical counterpart: two tectonic plates working against each other form a ridge, i.e. a mountain range; ice floes drifting against each other pile up and make a ridge; standing waves (both in water and in electronics) are ridges; a snowball is a ridge made of snowflakes. Many small particles being pressed into some shape: that is a ridge. A mental ridge is the result of two intentions of comparable magnitude flowing against each other, getting locked up and staying that way, with the result of indecision and the blockage of rational action. (The particles forming a mental ridge are minute quanta of mental energy. More of this in Part Two.)

An example: a man, out on the sea, falls overboard and drowns. He struggles against his death with all his might, i.e. he uses physical and mental energy to fight what's going on. This way a ridge is formed. It contains the information of what happened at the time of the contrasurvival incident. This information is recorded (and later played off) in the form of mental image pictures. Mental image "pictures" don't neccessarily appear visually but in the form of unwanted and inopportune thoughts, emotions, physical sensations and pains. In the example above: in his next lifetime this man may start feeling severely uncomfortable at the sight of water, get the thought of having to avoid boats in order to stay alive, feel the taste of salt water on his tongue and a choking feeling in his lungs anytime he sees a boat race on TV.

The information is fully there but not neccessarily available to be looked at due to the unconsciousness at the time it was received. (How information can be received despite the person's unconsciousness will be partly explained further down in this chapter and – in detail – in Part Two of this book.)

The engram, therefore, is a complete recording of a harmful incident. It consists of a ridge with pictures in it, some of which one can recall and others which are unconscious. An engram is the facsimile of the real event, a mental video recording. Pictures one cannot control are engram pictures. In order to erase them one has to find the basic incident and run all unconsciousness out of it. (For details on the procedure, see "Dianetics".)

So much on the picture making mechanism. With this understood it becomes quite apparent how one can snatch a picture away from another. A picture is not a "nothingness" but a "somethingness". It's a solid ridge. One can see it even: people whose ridges are restimulated and have come alive, look grey in the face and massy around the head or the body. Pictures can be looked at and grabbed at and pulled in and pushed out. They aren't visible to the naked eye and not touchable by one's naked hands, but mentally they can be perceived, yes, and handled. *"Thus your thetan has two things; he has his own record of real experience, of things which actually happened to him; and he has whole banks of "second facsimiles" or photographs he has taken from other thetan banks."* [5]

Pictures are not to be found in a person's head, by the way. You can't discover them by neurosurgery. They are part of the **mind** of man, not of his brain.

GENETIC MEMORIES

Hubbard made further discoveries. Apart from "home-made" pictures and "foreign-made" ones, yet another source of disturbance to the unsuspecting thetan was registered: pictures preserved in the genetic make-up of the body; pictures which tell the tale of the evolutionary development from mono-cell to homo sapiens. (Even here, the experience is not unique to scientology. Similar impressions are recorded by people in deep meditation or by those who took LSD in the 60's. They called it "cellular awareness".)

Genetic images tell of plankton washed ashore millions of years ago, of a shell with a sandgrain irritating its muscle, of fishes and birds being eaten by predators. Who made these pictures? Not the thetan himself. Very few thetans ever take animal or plant bodies and, if so at all, for a short time only. Having important things to do they usually choose the most advanced, the human form. Yet the thetan (in session) will recall pictures of this kind, and recalling and running them will alleviate his psychosomatic afflictions. So again: who made these pictures?

Hubbard found there is an agency in the body which collects pro- and contra-survival incidents on a cellular level. It is a *mental* agency which penetrates all the body cells; it is not a material recording device. In a way, we are dealing with a "created spiritual entity of a low order". Hubbard called it **Genetic**

Entity or **GE**. It acts like a "battery" feeding life energy into the body, or like a "computer programme" steering it. Without the GE, the body wouldn't survive when the thetan goes exterior – such as in deep sleep or in the unconsciousness during accidents or heavy operations. The GE's circuitry keeps the body going in the absence of the thetan.

The GE stores all information that has to do with the body: death and injury. Its primitive intelligence thinks in terms of avoidance only, in order that the organism may not be again exposed to the same dangerous circumstances. This way it aids its future survival. Impacts of sufficient magnitude and repetitiousness, picked up by the GE, therefore contribute to the shaping of the individual and the species in accordance with the environment. *"The genetic line consists of the total incidents which have occurred during the evolution of the mest body itself."* (Ch.4) *"It carries on through the evolutionary line, parallel with the protoplasmic line, generation for generation (. . .)"*(Ch.3) *"The GE continues as the guiding genius throughout prenatal life, building, regulating the heartbeat and attending to complex structural matters."* [5]

What exactly is an **entity**? Nothing but a ridge which – as goes with all ridges – contains the pictures of the time it was made. There are home-made and foreign-made entities, just as there are home- and foreign-made ridges. It's two words for the same thing. Different aspects are being emphasized, though: "Ridge" is a merely structural description; "entity" refers to the subjective experience of the person in question – who may perceive his entities as "demons", "ghosts", or "disembodied voices".

The Genetic Entity follows the same creation principle as any other entity, too. They are created by the totality of the body's theta when things were going rough. This "totality of the body's theta" isn't just one entity but a multitude of them – each having a specific task to do inside the body, each having its own timetrack, each with its own potential aberratedness due

31

to the engrams it has recorded. All in all they form what Hubbard, in "Dianetics", called the **somatic mind**. However, as all the entities of the somatic mind form a self-containing network, an "agency of their own", the term Genetic Entity (singular) has come to be used for it in the course of time. The way you experience it in session really makes you feel as if you were dealing with one single terminal only, not with an immense number of individual entities.

After death, quite some time after the thetan has withdrawn from the body, the GE will leave, too. A body which is attached to a life-saving machine for years and years, usually has been deserted by the thetan long ago already. It is run by the GE only. Once this body dies, the GE will go find a new body for itself. It practically never happens that the thetan meets again with a former GE of his. They run along separate time-tracks.

Looking at it structurally, we see that the thetan is not only "pushed around" by the foreign-made entities of others, but as well by the genetic entities of the body. He hangs in a network of criss-cross influences. He is not alone. "(. . .) *beings of the class of homo sapiens are composite beings motivated by a theta being, entities* (another term for ridges), *the GE and the environment.*" [5]

Fantastic as all of this may appear, these pictures *are* found by the auditor and they *are* traced down to their various sources by the pc: to his own track, another thetan's track, or the evolutionary track of the GE. Yet the ordinary person will be rather helpless concerning the proper evaluation and discrimination of the pictures streaming in on him, be it in or out of session. He may easily fall into the trap of thinking they were all his own. Therefore it is the task of the auditor, and a mark of his skill, to help the pc differentiate between the various sources of pictures so as to avoid the pc misidentifying an incident as his own when it isn't. A failure to do this may cause severe trouble for the pc and make the session stall.

Sanity, says Hubbard, is *"the ability to recognize differences, similarities and identities"* [2]. The more the auditor aids the pc to increase this ability, the more the pc will become causative over the phenomena of his mind, and the sooner he will be clear.

GAMES AT THE DAWN OF TIME

Let us sum up what has what has emerged so far: Man, as we saw, is not looked at as a body plus a brain; his existence is not seen as limited to one lifespan only. The term "thetan" was coined to describe him as an immortal being. As such he has existed before there were time and objects, i.e. physical "mest" (matter, energy, space and time). Even whilst having a body he does not neccessarily occupy it all of the time but may go exterior to it to the degree that he is in command of this ability. He works with mental mest in order to create intention beams, pictures and ridges.

This implies that man isn't only operating on a physical level but on a theta level, too. He is operating as a thetan, i.e. he creates effects by merely mental or spiritual means. Hubbard came to distinguish between "homo sapiens", i.e. man living on the level of mere physical awareness, and operating thetan or **OT**, i.e. man being aware of his immortality, his spiritual powers and his ability to use them. *"Operating Thetan – an individual who could operate totally independently of his body, whether he had one or didn't have one"* [2].

These findings are not a breathtaking novelty. They have always been in the awareness of man; to regain them was the objective of religious thought and practice since the days of the vedic hymns. Hubbard actually never claimed that he invented anything new but only used new words for old knowledge. *"For to say that out of whole cloth and with no background, a Westerner such as myself should suddenly develop all you need to know to do the things they were trying to do (in the East), is an incredible and an unbelievable and an untrue statement. (. . .) So, we combine the collective wisdom of those ages with a sufficient impatience and urgency. (. . .) Scientology carries forward a tradition of wisdom which concerns itself about the soul and the solution of mysteries of life. It has not deviated."* [6]

It was Hubbard's intention to rehabilitate the spiritual powers inherent in man. They were there before time was, and they are still there, simply because they are outside and above time. They cannot perish. But – given certain cultural circumstances – they may be ignored, belittled and laughed at and so one tends to invalidate their existence. Yet they can be rekindled easily – as may be demonstrated by various spiritual practices of which auditing is only one example.

There are two conclusions one may draw from the above. One is that, if a thetan can move from body to body as he desires, there is nothing to keep him from moving from planet to planet or indeed all around the innumerable galaxies of the physical universe. He may take his position (or body) anywhere. As he doesn't move by machinery but by his own will and purpose, he is not tied to lightspeed but travels at the speed of thought. Therefore it is at least thinkable that a certain proportion of Earth population actually consists of visitors from elsewhere – and that they came even without the neccessity of space travel. You couldn't tell by their bodies. We are talking of the thetans themselves who came. Their propositions may be quite different from each other – friendly or hostile, as the case may be. They surely didn't come without a reason. You, the reader, may be one of them!

Conclusion two: Once one accepts that there are pictures which weren't made by oneself (as the corresponding incidents didn't happen on one's own track but on that of others), the question arises as to how this mechanism can be used or misused. In present and recent times picking up other people's pictures has become a fairly incidental affair, something one doesn't particularly decide to have happen, as we saw in the example of Mrs.Dimple who had nightmares of getting stabbed to death. Pictures acquired this way may stay for a while and then go elsewhere or even thin out with use and fade away. Not so with the heavy-duty pictures made in times long gone, millions of years down the track. Back then thetans existed without bodies – to be specific: both you the reader and I the writer existed without bodies – and playing around with pictures was considered great fun and a great way, too, to control others. And so force fields were created and tractor waves and pressor waves used and all manner of theta energy traps were built in order to firmly install pictures in others to bring them under one's dominion. (A weak dramatization of this can be observed in the persistent efforts of advertment agencies to impress brand names and pictures upon the population. A more brutal dramatization is to be found in brainwashing. Both methods, compared to then, are gentle.)

This possibility of "invading and visiting thetans", "thetan wars" and "thetan games" already mentioned in 1952, were fully confirmed fifteen years later when Hubbard, in 1967, encountered powers from outside this planet blocking his attempts "to make OTs". Hubbard was not willing to take it with his hands down and, in his turn, prepared a galactic war by telepathic means. (More of this later on.)

SUMMARY

The "new view of man", what does it consist of? Of the idea that a person isn't made out of one piece but that he or she is "multivalent". Man is being affected by a multiplicity of spiritual influences; he is not neccessarily the master in his own house. In administrative terms, there are three "administrative levels" to a thetan with a body: the thetan, his entities and the GE. The body may be compared to a ship; the thetan to a captain who suffers under the burden of his past and keeps parts of it a secret. He drinks in order to forget. His officers (the entities) keep giving opinions and have nothing else in mind but becoming captain themselves – which is not difficult at all, as the old man is quite often in too foggy a state as to do his duty. Everytime the officers manage to take control of the ship, each one steers it his own way, and it goes in circles. The crew (GE) is following orders which have been derived from precedents over millions of years; they don't pay particular attention to the commands of the captain or the officers.

Within each administrative level there are horizontal communication lines; between levels there are vertical command lines. They are in poor shape, as one can easily imagine. Therefore there is a lot of gossip on each level, but there is no flow of orders from the top down and no feedback on the reverse route. The captain is utterly dependent on his crew. As soon as something unpleasant occurs (a restimulation), the whole ship knows about it within a few moments; the crew goes on strike or even mutinies. Naturally, given these circumstances, the captain has trouble keeping his ship on course. Small wonder that he becomes increasingly depressive towards the end of his career.

A Fateful Church

Between 1950 and 1954, times were good for Hubbard's movement. His lectures were attended by thousands of people, many of whom came from overseas. Auditors worked in hospitals and helped to speed up recovery. In California permission had been granted to establish a scientology university. (This scheme eventually failed.) Organisationally it was all held together by the HASI (Hubbard Association of Scientologists International) which consisted of Hubbard, a few staff and a large number of members, i.e. auditors, worldwide.

When you look at the amount of organisational policies written between 1950 and 1953, you can tell that Hubbard had an easy time: he wrote only two in total. His main concern was the development of "the tech" and its philosophical ramifications.

This was soon to change. In 1954 the Church of Scientology (CofS) was formed in Washington D.C. Now Hubbard was busy establishing it: in the five years between 1954 and 1959 he issued 180 policy letters. And there were more to come in the future.

Why he formed the CofS is open for argumentation. Some say it was purely for tax reasons, and they surely have a point there. But Hubbard must have had a bigger problem than that if he turned the simplicity of the HASI into the ever-growing complexity of the CofS. He probably needed an instrument to give him the legal stand to defend his movement against attacks.

Much as scientology had been steadily growing for a good four years already, dark clouds overshadowed its growth almost from the day it started. In 1950, one month after DMSMH had come out, the American Medical Association (AMA) declared Hubbard a nutcase. The World Federation of Mental Health (WFMH), the American Psychiatric Association (APA), the CIA – they all got busy investigating, supposing, opinionating, giving each other false or invented data, spreading rumours. In the course of an FBI investigation already in 1951, false reports were put into Interpol files and made available to all Interpol file users worldwide [7]. These data were used and re-used in press articles against scientology in the years to come. They were never doubted or put in question by those who used them.

This is peculiar insofar as dianetics (scientology didn't really exist yet) hadn't done any damage to anyone yet. Prices were none out of the ordinary, enthusiasm was generally high, Hubbard was about in person and spread a mood of bonhommie and scientific pioneer spirit. Every month brought new insights and advances which were communicated in magazines such as the "Dianetic Auditor's Bulletin", the "Journal of Scientology" and the "Professional Auditor's Bulletin", with Hubbard writing more busily than ever. There was a big happy family flair about it all. And it wasn't a "youth cult" at all, as the press had it: The majority of the participants were people in the healthy middle of their lives, professionals from various fields, good citizens.

Yet dianetics and (later) scientology *had* done something. By their mere existence they had stirred up embarrassments the organizations mentioned above would have preferred to keep well hidden. These ventilated their rage by accusing scientology – funnily enough – of the very things they were doing themselves.

Hubbard had asserted that most illnesses (70%) were psychosomatic and could be cured by auditing and not medicine. This went against the doctors; consequently the American Medical Association accused auditors of being quacks. He had asserted that drugs, hypnosis and electric shocks were not only unnecessary for therapy but actually harmful. This went against psychiatry; so the American Psychiatric Association accused scientologists of using drugs and hypnosis. He had made it a strong point that no violence ought to be used in the course of therapy. This went against the World Federation of Mental Health who protected even those psychiatrists who raped their female patients as part of "therapy"; so they accused scientologists of indulging in sex orgies. To top it up, Hubbard – by developing dianetics – had found a way of undoing brainwashing. Techniques which turned people into live robots by giving them instructions under the influence of pain, drugs and hypnosis, were a subject of major interest to the secret services in the 40's and 50's. Corresponding research projects were undertaken in the psychological faculties of universities all around the planet. The CIA in particular felt offended by Hubbard's dianetic techniques and – naturally – accused scientology of brainwashing. The whole scenario of mind control and large scale electronic population control was threatened to be uncovered by scientology auditors [7, 8, 9, 10]. These were enemies to be reckoned with. Hubbard saw it. The CofS was his answer to the threat – too weak an answer as it turned out. On United States territory, Hubbard didn't manage to hold his own against the enemy. In 1959 he went to England.

ESCAPE TO ENGLAND

Hubbard bought St.Hill Manor, an old manor house in Sussex near the town of East Grinstead. There things continued at an ever-expanding rate. By this time the CofS had gained a foothold in all English-speaking countries around the planet. St.Hill became – to scientologists internationally – the navel of the world. Hubbard continued researching and teaching. He only taught by lecture, backed up by summary write-ups called HCOBs (Hubbard Communications Office Bulletins) which – together with the magazines mentioned – were sent to auditors all around the world. His speeches and communications were almost exclusively addressed to the professional auditors and church executives of that time -which nowadays makes them almost unintelligible to outsiders or beginning students.

In the 50's and 60's there was no "paying public" in today's sense. There were only auditors, both professional and semi-professional, and they audited each other. Hubbard would give a lecture and propose a new process with the target in mind to find the fastest route to Clear. (He himself had made Clears since 1948. Now he tried to teach others to do it.) The auditors would sit down and run this process on each other: first one way to a result, then the other way. This was called co-auditing. To some extent, everyone internationally was participating in these projects. Telexes and letters were flying back and forth between St. Hill and the scientology organisations of South Africa, Australia, New Zealand and the US. Not that Hubbard took anyone's opinion or advice – he only relied on himself. But he needed everybody's results to determine what course to take in his research. In 1965 came his great breakthrough: Clears could be made by others than himself. He seemed to have wrapped it up.

Yet the enemy wasn't sleeping and Hubbard, with all the time he spent on his research, still kept a watchful eye on the movements of press and politics. He quipped that there were more FBI agents than students on the courses of some of the scientology organisations. Security became an issue. Staff were trained in a procedure called "security checking" to find infiltrators by means of the E-meter and clever questioning – yet some slipped through, as the future showed.

In 1963, the unexpected happened: the FBI raided the CofS organisation in Washington D.C., wrecked the furniture, threatened the staff and seized books, E-meters and auditing folders containing personal data of pcs. Similar things happened in Los Angeles. (The confiscated items were given back only many years later, after an extended legal battle.) In 1965, scientology was banned in the state of Victoria, Australia; this ban was then extended over all Australia and England, too. In England it concerned only foreign scientologists travelling into the country. They were turned back at the border. (In England, the ban was lifted in 1980.)

Hubbard obviously had a problem. The barriers seemed larger than his chances. In fact, the problem was threefold: One, governments and the press were against him. Two, some staff were disloyal to him and in fact in the service of the power groups mentioned earlier. Three, his loyal staff may have been willing, yes, but not neccessarily able to do the job – due to their unsuitable professional backgrounds. What Hubbard needed, were auditors, course supervisors and able administrators. What he got were butchers, bakers, engineers, nurses, musicians, secretaries, housewives, and some business people, too. Here he had a product (auditing) which was in growing demand despite certain efforts to suppress it, there he was lacking staff to deliver it. To cap it all, there wasn't even the time to train those who were there. It was all cope, stress and nervousness.

Things seemed to slip out of his hands. The house was on fire; Hubbard poured out policies, orders, telexes to smother the flames. Between 1960 and 1966 he issued 1000 "Hubbard Communications Office Policy Letters" (HCOPLs). Most of them were of three to five pages length. The items "suppressive persons" (SPs), "justice procedures" and "ethics handlings" ranged heavily in the foreground – understandable in the light of the tight situation scientology was in.

In 1966 a special branch was formed: the Guardian's Office (GO). It was to take care of all manner of outside aggressions so as to keep the organisations ("orgs") free to deliver uninhibitedly. The GO was established hierarchically and represented in each continent, each country and each org; St.Hill was the head office worldwide. Apart from its defensive duties the GO had the task of monitoring and investigating the doings of psychiatry, the FBI and the CIA, and expose them in the press. They did so in the manner of "investigatory journalism" and did a good job at it to start with. Much later, though, in the 70s, the GO network had become so much a machine in its own right that it overshot the mark and began dirty tricks campaigns on people they considered enemies to scientology. It didn't take much to make the GO think someone was a potential or active "suppressive person". On such persons blackmail, libel and slander, even personal threats and violence were used. The most insignificant press statement regarding scientology from the side of some Member of Parliament was sufficient to launch a full scale legal attack on him – which didn't help to heighten the public repute of the CofS [7, 9].

STAR WARS

Back to the year 1963: Hubbard worked out a twenty-six step "Plan for World Peace" involving the governments of Earth and the United Nations. Its major target was the abolishment of nuclear arms. This plan was meant to create a big agreement regarding the game of scientology amongst Hubbard's followers, something to set against the organizedness of the enemy forces. These he didn't see on Earth alone but in the galactic space around Earth. He was convinced that the real big bad boys were to found off the planet.

Neither Hubbard nor his auditors ever questioned extrasensory perceptions, even if they sounded like science fiction. They perceived a space battle going on with themselves – as "operating thetans" (OTs) – taking part in it by means of their telepathic energies.

Here follows a quotation of one of those policy letters which were thought to be "too hot" to be released to the general public. It shows how large Hubbard envisioned the game he considered himself a strategist in. He wrote it on June 25, 1963: *"When we were attacked in January for using E-meters, I adopted for us a 2 part policy: 1. To hold the line legally and win in courts where possible but in no event to lose ground, 2. To speed up research, bypassing Clear and Theta Clear as objectives (. . .) and concentrating on the attainment by auditing of the state of OT as the best forward answer to our difficulties. In part one of this programme, we are succeeding easily. But it is only short term and world deterioration is accelerating. In part two (. . .) we have OT in direct and real sight (. . .). We are then only months away from having OTs, a year at the most. The trouble with OTs in the past has only been lack of cooperation and a commonly agreed upon objective. Without these, OTs eventually fall prey again to smaller beings with bigger organization skill. (. . .) OT is an unstable state only when OTs are not cooperating with OTs. (. . .) The proof is, OTs have not survived as OTs whenever this superindividuation collided with the superorganization of weaker beings. (. . .) The answer is to remain organized (. . .). The first step is to prevent atomic war and planetary chaos and to utilize Earth as a rehabilitation centre since it has already had the technology established here. A second step following after would be to establish units not unlike central organizations (of scientology), in nearby systems. No real conflict with stellar powers interested in these areas will develop as I can vouch for the two most concerned in this galaxy, the Espinol United Stars to which the solar system distantly belongs and the Galactic Confederation to which Espinol moderately bows. (. . .)"*

No matter what you and I may think about these lines, Hubbard was convinced of their truth. With this program the starting signal for a crusade without compare was given. It was Hubbard and his OT auditors against a world seen as infested by infiltrators from outer space and their dirty politics here on Earth.

The above quotation contains a sentence of great significance for the future application of the tech. It is the statement that the one target to be followed at that time was the making of OTs and that all earlier targets were to neglected. These consisted of a step-by-step clearing program: Clear as freedom from one's case and Theta Clear as freedom from any tie to the body. From now on the furthering of the individual in the direction of his ultimate spiritual freedom was not the guiding line; instead all forces available were to be utilized for a battle which in Hubbard's opinion was to decide over the collapse of the world or its salvation. As many people as possible were to be rehabilitated regarding their "OT-ness". The "case" of the person, his degree of "clearness" seemed – in this state of emergency – less important than developing his spiritual powers and adding them to the common cause. The neccessary study materials were to be released in 1967 only and not, as expected, within a year. The spirit of this state of emergency, lasting for years, was to determine the CofS for decades to come. They haven't recovered from it up to the present day. "Go OT, no matter at what cost!" still is the widely proclaimed motto.

In the course of this mobilization the outside pressures (both planetary and, as Hubbard saw it, extra-planetary) had increased to such a point that St.Hill didn't seem safe any longer. Hubbard once again had to seek refuge elsewhere: this time in the un-governed waters outside the five-mile zone off the European coastlines.

OFF TO THE HIGH SEAS

What follows now are the ten adventurous years of the Sea Organisation (1967-1977). Hubbard bought a medium-sized passenger ship, named it "Apollo" and continued his research whilst cruising the Mediterranean Sea. Later two more ships were added to the fleet. The Apollo, with Hubbard as Commodore, was the Flag Ship. All staff of the Sea Organisation (or SO) had naval ranks apart from their post name or auditor qualification. Prior to starting the "Sea Project" (as it was called in its formative stage), Hubbard had resigned from the CofS as Executive Director and took the title "Foun der" instead, holding himself available for consultation and signatures, though. *"On specific request, as a writer, I will write books on Scientology, its organization, and will write HCOBs* (bulletins) *and policy letters as requested."* This he said in a policy of September 6, 1966. What it meant, in actual fact, is that he ran the CofS by telex, from the ship. By request only, yes, but he ran it. Maybe not because he wanted to but because he had to. None of the executives replacing him were up to the size of the task. Hubbard had to step in whenever the house caught fire again, and it did that often.

Mismanagement and organizational stupidity from the side of the org staffs on land were the daily, weekly and monthly mishap of the orgs internationally, resulting in loss of income, legal battles, internal tensions and bizarre solutions. Already in February 1965 Hubbard was less than charmed by his church. He didn't put all the blame on enemy attacks but found enough fault amongst his followers to say: *"Trouble spots occur only where there are 'no results'. Attacks from governments or monopolies occur only when there are 'no results' or 'bad results'. (. . .) So the ogre which might eat us up is not the governement or the High Priests. It's our possible failure to retain and practise our technology."* [11] Nevertheless, the CofS kept growing. Not that it went smooth as silk; it was rough. Hubbard poured his administrative resourcefullness into yet another few hundred policy letters, with the emphasis on ethics, security and "admin know-how" (as he called it).

Despite all precautions the powers which were determined to squeeze the life out of scientology eventually got at the Apollo itself. The ship did not escape the long arm of the combined intrigue and rumour machines of CIA and Interpol. Already in 1969 it had started to be banned from various harbours; in the end it became so bad that the Sea Org had no place left to go to [7]. Meanwhile, though, – due to various successes on the legal front – it had become safe again to go on land in the US. The Flag Ship plus crew went to Florida in 1977; the Fort Harrison, a large old hotel in the town of Clearwater, was bought for a few million dollars cash; the Sea Org staff moved in. The place was then called "Flag", to symbolize that the Flag Ship had moved on land. To church scientologists, "Flag" ever since – and even after the death of Hubbard – stands for: this is the place where the Commodore himself is present, be it in body or in spirit; this is the place where scientology tech is delivered at the highest possible standard. They call it the "Mecca of standard tech", and they are dead serious about it. The "navel of the world" had wandered from St.Hill via the Mediterranean to Clearwater, Florida.

STAR WARS EXPANDED

With respect to Hubbard's research, the Sea Org years had resulted in a major shift of viewpoint concerning the nature of the "case" (i.e. the sum of engrams and ridges a person has in restimulation), and concerning the nature of the persecution scientology and Hubbard himself were exposed to. It was a shift not in principle but in emphasis.

His hope to make OTs soon (voiced in the 1963 policy quoted) hadn't come true as soon as he had expected. It had in fact taken till 1967. The research on the matter had actually started with Hubbard investigating the trouble his Clears were running into. For themselves, they were doing fine; they had no attention on their own past; all woes and troubles had been discharged; they were masters of their own mental energies and masses. Yet mental pictures and energies, not caused by them, afflicted them. Much as they felt the influence they couldn't spot its source.

A Clear is, by definition, a single being with no self-created masses or ridges attached to him. If he isn't doing well there must be something influencing him which he himself did not create and which is beyond his normal perception of foreign-made entities. Some extensive exploratory auditing (on Hubbard and on others) revealed that ridges had been installed on Earth to make this planet a trap for any thetan who would take a body here. The trap was set in such a way that the person would follow the pictures contained in the ridges as if by command, and that he wouldn't be able to ever leave Earth again on his own account. These pictures and masses were not only found by Hubbard but by his auditors, too. After having located and run them, Clears would find their troubles disappearing. Therefore Hubbard concluded that there must be truth to the matter. He investigated further.

Looking at his findings – as you will see them summarized in a moment – one is likely to wonder whether he didn't get mixed up with his own science fiction fantasies. Hubbard himself, though, and the people who were part of the research, would have sworn any oath that they had not deviated even a fraction of an inch from their personal sanity and integrity, no matter what anyone else may think.

With this word of warning, here is the story: The scheme for the trap set for the thetans on this planet goes back to a galactic confederation which consisted of 21 suns and 76 planets. Its ruler, Xenu, attempted to gain control over all beings under his rule by **implanting** his own intentions into their minds. "Implanting" means installing attitudes and opinions into another by the use of force, drugs, electric shocks or a combination of the three. It's something like brainwashing, only worse. These implants contained pictures and commands on the use of sex, drugs, violence and religious symbols; their purpose was to produce aberrated behaviour concerning these subjects, in man.

This incident happened 75 million years ago. There were bodies, cars, machines like today except on an incredibly high level of technical accomplishment. The style and taste of those days corresponds to the thirties of this century. Xenu tried to "solve" the overpopulation prevailing then by having people mass drugged, killed and – as thetans – transported to Earth. This happened to billions and billions of thetans. To finish off, Earth itself was blasted into oblivion by H-bombs being dropped down volcano craters.

To Hubbard, this incident is *the* basic engram on the time track of Earth. According to him, all people who ever lived on Earth were affected by it either directly or indirectly, all history shaped by it, all culture contaminated by it. He sees the ridges generated during this genocide and subsequent implant being dramatized in the fear of overpopulation – demonstrated by propaganda against large families and deliberately kept up starvation; in population control by drugs; in mass evacuations and the slaughtering of whole populations; in brainwashing as a weak edition of implanting; in the suicidal play with and in the panic of, atomic weapons. The whole idea behind the implant (says Hubbard) is to make Earth population imitate the technical civilization of 75 million years ago and then trigger mankind to commit planetary suicide by means of the very technical advances they have achieved.

If one were to follow his line of thought, one would be bound to interpret certain cultural phenomena in a different light than usual. Take, for example, religious art. It seems that the mental image pictures Hubbard found as part of the implant appear on traditional paintings in the form of trumpeting angels and chariots ploughing through clouds, or in the hallucinations anchorites are tempted by. They appear in Tibetan meditation illustrations and in the custom of nailing people to the cross – as the Romans did two thousand years ago and as Australian aborigines still do (ritualistically) up to this day. C.G. Jung's study on "archetypes" could be interpreted as related to them.

In the second half of the 20th century the restimulators parallelling the contents of the incident are – for the first time in 75 million years – extant again on Earth: cars, airplanes, helicopters, telephones, wireless communication, space missiles, atomic bombs, hallucinogenic drugs, brainwashing, and electric shocks used in psychiatric "therapy" and death sentences. All the "dynamite charges" man has in his mind have been put by him in his environment and are working back on him. The planetary suicide program has started triggering itself. *"If you were looking for Hell and found Earth, it would certainly serve. War, famine, agony and disease has been the lot of Man. Right now the great governments of Earth have developed the means of frying every Man, Woman and Child on the planet.* (He is referring to the atom bomb.) *(. . .) We're not playing a minor game in Scientology. It isn't cute or something to do for lack of something better. The whole agonized future of this planet, every Man, Woman and Child on it, and your own destiny for the next endless trillions of years depend on what you do here and now with and in Scientology. This is a deadly serious activity. And if we miss getting out of the trap now, we may never again have another chance"* [11].

So much on the cultural history of Earth as interpreted by Hubbard. How serious he was about it can be seen in the fact that he didn't limit himself to philosophical musings about the matter. He saw his day-to-day physical and political doings menaced in direct consequence of Xenu's doings.

Hubbard already took it for granted that a thetan – i.e. the person as a spiritual being – was immortal and that his goals and intentions would not cease to exist at the point of body death but would last until they were either fulfilled or cancelled, no matter how many lifetimes it might take. This thought plus the newly discovered knowledge about the implant incident led Hubbard to the conclusion that Xenu and his men must be just as alive (on Earth or elsewhere) as Hubbard and his men and that Xenu probably never dropped his intention to win the world – an intention running diametrically counter to Hubbard's plan of "clearing the planet". And where would Xenu's men best take their bodies in present time (strategically speaking), if not in positions as close to Hubbard as possible? – All of a sudden it had to be taken into account that the whole CofS was infiltrated by Xenu's men; that things weren't limited to the undercover agents of the FBI.

By his very discoveries and results with regard to auditing, Hubbard had become a countercheck to Xenu's plot. As a consequence of his findings, he saw himself confronted with the pressing question: Who of the staff is a friend, who belongs to the enemy? Apparently, to find out about the true identity of the staff or the public it wasn't enough to check into the background of their present lives; one had to look deeper: what did they do 75 million years ago? Which party did they belong to then?

Hubbard and his staff went paranoid over this question and the threat posed thereby. The typical characteristics of today's CofS – strict command abidingness, military/naval toughness, blind followership, preparedness to sniff an enemy every which way, paranoia – are all a remnant of those days.

It was in keeping with the matter at hand that the weapon Hubbard devised was a telepathic one. Obviously one cannot fight a thetan who points ridges, pictures, intentions and energy beams at one, with one's bare hands. Consequently the auditing processes Hubbard designed were to detect and undo the influence from other planets and spaceships, be they directed on Earth in general or certain individuals in particular.

"OPERATING THETANS"

The processes countering Xenu's schemes were named the "OT levels", ranging from OT I to OT III. (Further OT levels, for different purposes, were developed later.) Doing the OT levels was comparable to joining the partisan army, the guerrilla, and going to war. One didn't do it for "casegain" (i.e. to feel better personally) but for "clearing the planet". One felt sworn in to a common supra–individual cause. To start with, the OT levels were only delivered on the Flag Ship. The battle cry of the Sea Org was: "first this planet, then this sector of the galaxy, then the universe."

Naturally, rehabilitating one's higher spiritual dimensions has positive and pleasant aspects, such as conversing with well-meaning beings in spheres outside the physical universe, re-establishing connections with friends of ages ago who one thought were lost to one but in fact happen to live on this planet, too, and experiencing the coming and going of representatives of peaceful powers. They aren't *all* bad, out there, after all. The above Sea Org motto reveals, however, how much such positiveness had become sacrificed to a fighting mentality of "we are the only ones, the knights in white armour, the cavalry rescuing the fort". – Even though this mentality – in the light of the events to come – might be considered justified, it still put an ungoodly bias on the attitudes the staff identified with.

To the public things were made to look different. The longer the term OT was used for marketing and sales purposes the more its original meaning was twisted; eventually it came to mean something like a boosted-up version of superman. Those believing in this version of the word hoped to gain wondrous powers by doing the OT levels I to III, like walking on water, lifting objects by sheer intention, creating things out of thin air. They projected all their magic fantasies into this legend-embroidered state of OT. Of course, the disappointment was great. But as church registrars always were very skilled, as the public always was ready to believe that their dreams would finally come true, and as "ethics officers" always made very sure that no word about anyone's frustrations would leak out, the OT levels sold very well. "Going OT" – that meant finding the holy grail, attain enlightenment, disappear in some glorious nirvana. In the CofS, it is advertised in this manner up to the present day.

Hubbard himself was much more realistic than his adherents about the effects he would create with scientology. The OT levels were to free the individual from the pictures and masses imposed on him by Xenu's network. Disentangling oneself naturally went along with weakening the network. The end phenomenon for the individual was: free of the entanglement; the end phenomenon for the planet: a clear planet, i.e. one not governed by foreign intentions, pictures and energies.

Much as Hubbard loved to postulate and hypothesize what "a thetan in good shape" might be able to do (it would make any kind of superman blanche), he was as well very down-to-earth regarding the actual results to be expected from auditing. *"If you think for a moment that it's the purpose of Scn to produce something intensely spectacular like a ghost that can move cigarette paper or mountains, you have definitely gotten the wrong idea. We are interested in well men, we are interested in people with well bodies, who can think straight, and who co-operate on optimum solutions. We are not making magicians."* [12] *"We are not trying to achieve the certainty of mysticism, necromancy, or, to be blunt, the Indian ropetrick. We are trying to make sane, well beings."* [13] To Hubbard, what counted in the end, was the day-to-day performance of a person, his ability "to make it go right". Auditing on the OT levels certainly was one facet of life but by no means all there was to it.

"STANDARD TECH"

During the Sea Org years, apart from the discovery of earthly and not-so-earthly attacks and counterattacks, Hubbard had started to formulate what he thought was going to be his legacy concerning the tech. In 1968, on the ship, he gave a series of lectures, called the "Class VIII Course" (i.e. for auditors of this classification), which were to be the final word on the subject of auditing. After OT III there were seemingly no secrets left. From now on the tech was considered "standard", meaning that there was a minutely prescribed way to go about it which would not tolerate any deviations. All cases seemed solveable in accordance with a set pattern.

Why would Hubbard, himself the most unorthodox and "unruly" of all auditors, have constructed a corset like this? – Probably to somehow transfer his mastership to his pupils. In order to fully appreciate the neccessity for this new concept of "standard tech", one has to recognize how numerous the auditing procedures of 1968 had become, compared to the days of the Dianetics book (1950). Eighteen years of "streamlining" (Hubbard's term) had brought about a great number of individual auditing processes. In order to resolve the problems of his clients and answer the questions of his auditors, Hubbard forever had to come up with new solutions. They were distributed worldwide in the form of "Hubbard Communications Office Bulletins" and attained – as words of the master – the status of sacred untouchability. They were to be used as model solutions for each and every case problem coming up in session. In the end there were so many of them that the resulting complexity made the tech incomprehensible. Standard tech was Hubbard's answer to this state of affairs. The wild growth of processes from the past eighteen years was cut down to the most relevant ones. These were put in an order, brought into a strict and unvarying sequence and from here on out formed the steps of the "bridge". It was supposed to take any person from "green pc" to OT, like on an assembly line.

Impressive as this technological structure may appear in theory, it soon showed its drawbacks when it came to practical aplication. The flexibility, the raw man-to-man approach of Book One ("Dianetics") auditing gave way to an unwavering ridgidity. Auditing stopped being the solution-finding dialogue between two people and was turned into a ritualistic exercise, an application of rote procedures to all and sundry.

This future development of course was not expected to happen, when standard tech was proclaimed in 1968. All cases were thought to be solveable in a standard way and all pcs to get the same treatment wherever they went to get their auditing. These assumptions, as it turned out, were far from true. The tech had *not* been brought in its final form. Hubbard had to keep on correcting and corrrecting and issuing bulletin upon bulletin for the next ten years – till 1978. Pc's were *not* receiving standard tech wherever they went; there were in fact vast quality differences between orgs which enfuriated Hubbard to no small degree. Hubbard himself of course could do it all and was famous for it, so apparently the tech was good enough. The weak links in its transmission were the course rooms. Course supervisors – and therefore the auditors trained by them – were not always able to grasp Hubbard's technical and philosophical concepts and apply them sensibly. Hubbard countered this with the development of "study tech". Its success was limited. In the end it as well fell prey to the all-prevailing woodenness of application. As a side product the rather awkward "scientologist's jargon" developed, much to the annoyance of outsiders and new-comers.

Despite these unfavourable circumstances, the tech still worked on people. It led staff and public to the recognition of innermost certainties and spiritual enhancement. One just knew that the tech was correct and that one would progress more by further use of it.

BACK ON LAND

The Sea Org years, as we saw before, ended in 1977 when the Sea Org moved into the Fort Harrison. Hubbard stayed in hiding from his real and not-so-real enemies (he didn't appear in public any more and lived in forever changing secret locations); OT III was the hot and whispered-about magic level; the CofS aspired to become a world-embracing business set-up, ready to fight anyone by telepathic, legal or illegal means.

The tech certainly worked; people had life-changing gains from it. Its quality varied considerably, though, depending on the org and on the auditor. Yet the internal group-cohesiveness and the promotional machine of the CofS allowed no criticism: scientology was great, auditing a heavenly experience, and Flag was best of all. The church was always right, no matter how much an individual would be wronged by it. Staff who somehow didn't make it "went by the boards", i.e. were declared trouble sources or suppressive, and forgotten. The pc's whose cases for some reason didn't straighten out easily, soon filled the role of guinea pigs on which auditors could test their abilities. In case of failure they were handed over to the next higher org, there to have some more money drained out of them. For such people it was not unusual to accumulate a dozen or more session folders – a stack reaching up the ceiling. Several hundreds of valuable auditing hours were churned out on them with no result. In the end, when there was no further bright idea as to what to do next, the unfortunate victims of such experimentation found the blame put on themselves: the CofS quite haughtily found that they weren't "up to it" yet – and dismissed them as "potential trouble sources". The originally playful spirit of the 50s was degenerating into a super-serious no-fun thought regimen under the domination of a mammoth machine who had nothing in mind but to take possession of the planet. "Clearing the planet" came to be understood as: "We are the only ones who know anything about anything, so you'd better listen to us, buddy!"

The Church of Scientology, within twenty-five years, had turned into a self-adulatory insider club of naval attire and fascist performance who shunned all comparison with the outside world and only applauded its own self-created values. Hubbard lived in hiding; his only contact with the CofS were communicators who increasingly started to control his communication lines and thereby controlled *him*. His power had gone over to the apparatus he had built over the years; it had become bigger than him.

Unaware of it all, staff and public loved Hubbard more than ever; the PR machine made him come across as everybody's best friend. "Do as Ron says" was the order of the day in whatever difficult situation. This made for meticulous study of source materials and ready quotations at any given moment, but it didn't make for good common sense thinking. The more the CofS moved away from its founder and became a machine in its own right, the more it lost in spirit and gained in stalinistic personality cult with all that goes along with it: handclapping in front of the photograph of the founder, telling anecdotes and legends about him, making his work their gospel. A system of mutual control made sure that nobody broke out of the system. Anyone who had negative feelings would push them out of his mind and feel guilty about them. After all, around here they are only doing what Ron says, and it must be right because Ron is always right. That was the simple logic which very effectively kept things together.

The more Hubbard receded as a person, the more "Ron" or "LRH" (L.Ron Hubbard) was sold to the public as a piece of merchandise. The "Old Man" never ceases to be there – portrayed, photographed, cast in bronze. He serves well as a sales gimmick. After 1980 he disappeared for good and lived in seclusion on a California ranch, kept incommunicado by the "communicators" controlling him. He died – so the CofS says – in 1986, aged 75.

Religious Salesmanship

Despite all the things one could say say against the CofS, one thing is for sure: they managed to keep going as a worldwide business and presenting themselves in the form of flashy buildings, glossy magazines, and pompous "Flag Events". If one is to believe their promotional campaigns, they are now, in 1990, in a better condition than ever before.

To look back: 1968 marked the arrival of standard tech. In 1970 the complete collection of Hubbard's policy letters was brought out in book form (ten volumes). In 1975 a glossary of scientology terms was issued, the "Technical Dictionary". 1976 brought the compact edition of the technical bulletins (twelve volumes). The years of improvisation were over. With regard to tech delivery, the CofS seemed all set to go off like a rocket. Yet with Hubbard gone (1980) and dead (1986) there was no-one to guide the mammoth with a spiritual goal in mind, therefore its only purpose became making money. In the course of the ten years after the withdrawal of the founder (1980 to 1990), the CofS found ever new ways to pull money out of people's pockets by putting new courses and new "rundowns" (i.e. auditing processes) as a must for everybody, on the curriculum. This curriculum – on the training side – is a sequence of courses one must do in order become an auditor; on the auditing side it is "The Bridge to Total Freedom".

According to Hubbard in 1968, standard tech consists of finding the shortest route between the entry point of the person on the "Bridge" and the state of Clear. The seventies saw a change in this; in the eighties this concept was thoroughly abolished. Today everyone is shoved through the same routine whether they need it or not, with the excuse that "Ron says so". Which means nothing but profiteering on the personal need and good faith of one's customers. But people pay, and put up with anything. They are scared "to lose their Bridge" and burn in hell forever. It seems they would rather sacrifice their personal integrity than relinquish their OT levels.

Regarding "tech delivery", Flag – up to this day – functions as the senior technical org from where the tech is monitored internatioally. Organizationally, there is "International Management" ("Int") in Los Angeles from where seven top executives are calling the shots. "Int" runs scientology orgs worldwide by direct orders given through telex machines. Their common objective is "to get the stats up". ("Stats" is short for statistics.) The stats for the week are counted each Thursday at 2pm. This means high-pressure time for all staff. It means pushing students through courses no matter whether they have grasped the materials or not, sqeezing the last possible auditing hour out of each auditor and pc in sight, "regging" (the registrar selling services) more money than the week before etc. Even a single "Dianetics" paperback sold literally in the last minute to the odd passer-by on the street would save the neck of some hard-struggling staff member. If need be, he would even buy the book himself! – Whoever's stats aren't up by Thursday 2pm is in for trouble: in additon to his 70 hour week he has to put in overtime to make up the damage.

It's a high pressure system based on fear and slave labour. The euphemistic motto is: "high purpose low pay". The material existence of most staff looks like it: long hours in exchange for mere pocket money. This demonstrates how well the indoctrination machine works.

There are two types of staff. Contracted staff go on time contracts of two-and-a-half or five years. Sea Org recruits sign a billion year contract. Of course it is purely symbolic and has no legal value, but it is taken as seriously as any blood oath in the tribal days of pagan Europe. The benefit of staff getting the "bridge" for free or at least at half price (depending on the auditing level) is a reason for many to join staff. Which is not to say that they get very far with it. Once a staffmember is "recruited", he is trained for his post, be it in the "technical division" (auditing and training) or in an administrative division. When he has finished studying for his post, when his stats are up, when he can make some hours in his day to get sessions, and when just at those hours there is an auditor free for him (the paying public always has priority), then and only then may one staff member or the other, in the course of some years, make it up to Clear. When he is lucky. Not many of them are.

The Sea Org, after it moved on land, became a harbour for anyone who didn't quite know what to do with himself and his life. Sea Org recruits, over the years, became increasingly younger. The paying public certainly couldn't be labelled by the term "youth cult" but the Sea Org staff well deserves this name. Although the Sea Org has been on land since 1977, men and women alike still have naval ranks and walk around in blue uniforms and white captain's hats. In the seventies and eighties, the SO staff member lived crammed into dark quarters, for example in the cellar near the ventilation ducts, in the otherwise not lettable rooms of cheapest boardinghouses, or in a dormitory shared with at least as many people as would be considered bearable in a refugee camp. He had about four square meters to his name. He got up early, worked all day, came home late and only in order to sleep. (Which is why four square meters were all he needed). He worked six and a half or seven days a week depending on how his stats were last Thursday. His pay was likely to not exceed 15 Dollars a week for many months in a row. Parents had an hour or two "family time" per day; children grew up rough as wild ponys in internally run kindergartens (if available), their ears full with Sea Org jargon and four letter swear words. (It was considered becoming to swear, for gentlemen and ladies alike.)

International Management is assisted in its tasks by a number of administrative networks: the Commodore Messenger Org, the LRH Communicators network, the Flag Representative network, the Watchdog Committee, the Religious Technology Center, the Guardian's Office, etc. Some of these networks are established on a purely international level, others reach down to continental, national and city org levels.

The "tech orgs" must make money, make money, make money. In an "admin org" whose target it is to make the technical orgs make money, the jingle is slightly different: make them make money, make them make money, etc etc.

All money for the weekly overheads and staff pay has to be made each week in a new unit of time, by the auditors and course supervisors alone. Auditing and training (apart from book sales) are the only income making activities in a scientology organization. Yet when one looks at the overall ratio between admin staff and tech staff one finds it to be something to the order of 17:1! One auditor or supervisor must feed seventeen admin staff members – of his own and of other (admin) orgs. Small wonder staff pay is low.

What step would such a waterlogged mammoth naturally take to preserve its survival? Raise the prices, of course. And so it happened. Starting in 1976 and continuing for a good ten years, the prices went up by 5% *per month.* (In England 10%.) It was started by Hubbard himself as the prices at the time needed adjusting. But Hubbard, in the late 70's, had already lost his grip on the church. And the prices kept climbing, climbing, climbing. (Even at present they climb occasionally.) And the public? They panicked – and bought on the basis of bank loans. They bought scores of auditing hours in advance and dozens of courses, just to beat the price rise.

A CHURCH EATING ITS CHILDREN

What makes people endure all this and go along with it? With some, it's the deep conviction that scientology is a good thing no matter how mad an executive may go occasionally and that one has to live through it till better days are around. To this type of people – usually Sea Org members – supporting scientology is worth more than their lives. With others (the public), the fear of losing their spiritual salvation stands in the foreground. "Going up the Bridge" is their one hope and goal for this life, believing without question that scientology is the one and only way to achieve their total spiritual freedom from the entrapment of compulsive reincarnation on this planet. The outlook of being declared a suppressive person (i.e. being excommunicated) to them is worse than any rudeness, degradation or injustice any ethics officer may dish out anywhere.

The CofS has started taking Hubbard literally, to value his every statement as supremely important, to not look at his general intention any more. In the 50s, by the pressure of necessity, the church was created by Hubbard as a weapon. By the end of the 70's it started to gain its own momentum. In the 80's it took on a colour of its own, moved away from the intentions of its creator and finally turned against its own members.

In 1982 the so-called "Finance Police" from International Management travelled around the planet and extorted huge sums from individual scientology missions for alleged "finance crimes" against the orgs. A "mission" is a privately owned center franchised to deliver certain standard scientology services. Mission holders were ordered to Flag, the Florida headquarters, to get expensive "security checking" for crimes they had allegedly committed. Some actually were declared a "suppressive person" on the spot by "finger declare" – i.e. by some Sea Org officer pointing his finger at them and "saying the word". (Officially, according to church policy, a thourough investigation should have been done.) Many missions broke down financially, never to recover again. Thousands of scientologists, both staff and public, were declared suppressive or simply left the CofS in protest.

The next move: the Religious Technology Center (RTC) was formed by a handful of top CofS executives. It had not been announced by Hubbard with a policy letter as one was accustomed to. The story goes that – in order to make up a proper charter – they forged LRH's signature. With the RTC, these few executives gained access to all of the CofS funds, reserves and resources and thereby to the peak power position in an international multimillion dollar enterprise.

In the years following the RTC coup the magazines became glossier, the promotion flashier, and the self-celebrations of the CofS more bloodcurdlingly embarrassing than ever. The decisive thing, though, started by the RTC and unheard of before, was the introduction of trademarks to make "Scientology Religious Technology" an industrial product comparable to Coca-Cola (a comparison cherished by church officials.) "Scientology" has come to be packaged up in the form of courses or bits of "Bridge". If it's bought in the Church of Scientology, it's the real thing. If it's bought elsewhere it cannot be but mere tinsel; it will be an alteration of the pure "standard" form. It must be, because only "suppressive" practitioners would use scientology without being in the CofS, and suppressive means insane, incapable, or worse, evil.

Scientology, defined by its founder as an "applied religious philosophy" has become a trademarked article subjected to an international PR- and marketing machinery which has no other intention than to make money out of the legacy of L.Ron Hubbard. His books, his taped lectures are marketed in ever new wrappings, the E-meter is priced at many times the value the actual device has, and the writings of Hubbard are shuffled about and put together in ever new courses and auditing run-downs. According to the CofS price list of November 1990 the auditing hour costs between 560 and 740 Dollars; they are sold in blocks of twelve-and-a-half hours only. For the E-meter you pay 4625 Dollars. And all these things are sold, sold, sold.

A summary of trademarks always appears in small print at the bottom of CofS promotional materials: "CSI LOGO (Church of Scientology International), SCIENTOLOGY, SCIENTO-LOGIST, DIANETICS, LRH (L.Ron Hubbard), OT, FREE-WINDS (the name of their cruise liner), FLAG, THE BRIDGE, HUBBARD, HCO, NEW ERA DIANETICS, the SCIENTOLOGY cross, the OT symbol, the LRH signature, E-METER, TRUTH REVEALED, the SCIENTOLOGY symbol, and the DIANETICS symbol are trademarks and service marks owned by the Religious Technology Center and are

used with its permission. (. . .) SCIENTOLOGY is an applied
religious philosophy." – Quite obviously the RTC are aspiring
to have the monopoly on scientology.

Who is running the show? – The answer is provided by a 12-
page glossy colour-brochure entitled "Total Expansion in the
1990's". The caption under a photo showing the seven chief
executives of the CofS reads: "International Executives, spea-
kers at the New Year's event in Los Angeles. From left to right:
Commander (Right Arm) Norman Starkey, Trustee of LRH
Estate; Ensign Heber Jentzsh, President of the Church of
Scientology International; Captain Mark Ingber, Comman-
ding Officer of the Commodore's Messenger Org International; Captain David Miscavige, Chairman of the Board Religious Technology Center; Captain Guillaume Lesevre, Executive Director International; Captain Marc Yager, Inspector General for Administration RTC; Captain Ray Mithoff, Inspector General for Technical RTC."

Notwithstanding its huge sales the CofS always managed to
keep its status of "non-profit organization". Legal attacks
proved fruitless. In addition to the profits it makes as a "non-
profit" organization it as well makes "real" profit through two
profit-oriented companies. One is officially only "associated"
but is in truth the fully dependent publishing house "New Era
Publications". The other is "Authors Services International" or
ASI. The only author who ever had the pleasure of receiving
their services, is Ron Hubbard. Here the marketing of the li-
cences for his scientological work as well as for his earlier
science-fiction writings is done. The money made winds up in
the pockets of those members of the Board of Directors of the
Church of Scientology who happen to be at the same time in
the directorate of the ASI. – It therefore appears that not all
Sea Org members get a mere pittance for their hard work.

The CofS has effectively become an instrument to suppress the
humanitarian and helpful aspects of scientology. There is no
need for any governement action or press campaign against
scientology. Left to their own devices, the Church of Scien-

tology will reliably pervert the subject to a point where it will become unbearable even to its members and it will disappear from the face of the Earth. In this context it is worth noting that the CofS, since the 50s, has kept publishing books by L.Ron Hubbard which were not actually written by him. It continues to do so even now, years after the death of the writer. They are the product of an editorial team as one can sometimes tell from the small print on the impressum page. But their sources stay hidden. There are no references as to what source materials were used. And whoever happens to know the relevant passages in the original text, can't help noticing how they were changed.

Those who may fear that the corrosion of source materials finally has set in, fear too late: staff who were working close to Hubbard at the time have witnessed that as early as 1973 technical bulletins (HCOBs) were written by others than Hubbard but issued under his name. And today, now that the RTC own the name "L.Ron Hubbard" as a trademark, there is of course no shortage of "sensational new manuscripts" by the late founder.

(You may wonder how the top brass of the CofS apparently have not benefitted from the improving practices of scientology. The criticism may be made that scientology does not work, but the simplicity seems to be that they never received much auditing or tech training, and because of having been brought up as Sea Org children, they never got a broad experience of life.)

HUBBARD'S COMMENTS

What might Hubbard have said about the matter? He actually foresaw the development decades earlier already and made some pointed remarks about it. In his "Essay on Management", of August 1951, he says: *"(. . .) most managements prefer a good, safely dead goal finder whose ideas and rationale are solidly held by the group, and most groups prefer live goal finders because as long as the goal finder lives (. . .), the group has a solid champion."* [14] – Small wonder the CofS never forgets to add an abundance of eversmiling Hubbard photos to their promo materials. Creating the impression that the goal finder still lives makes for better sales.

In contrast to the current CofS management Hubbard himself didn't think it was a good idea to monopolize his techniques. In "Dianetics" he says: *"Dianetics is not in any way covered by legislation anywhere for no law can prevent one man sitting down and telling another man his troubles, and if anyone wants a monopoly on dianetics, be assured that he wants it for reasons which have to do not with dianetics but with profit."*

As well in "Dianetics", Hubbard even asks scientologists to assist him in the future improvement of scientology methods: *"In twenty or a hundred years the therapeutic technique which is offered in this volume will appear to be obsolete. Should this not prove to be the case , then the author's faith in the inventiveness of his fellow man will not have been justified. (. . .) The application methods cannot but be refined. All sciences begin with the discovery of basic axioms. They progress as new data is discovered and as the scope of the science is widened. Various tools and techniques rise up continually, improved and re-improved. The basic axioms, the initial discoveries of dianetics are such solid scientific truths that they will be altered but little. (. . .)"* He ends on the words: *"In this handbook we have the basic axioms and a therapy which works. For God's sake, get busy and build a better bridge!"*

He demanded that men in general *"(. . .) have inalienable rights to think freely, to talk freely, to write freely their own opinions and to counter or utter or write upon the opinions of others."* The individual scientologist in particular is expected to *"use the best I know of Scientology to the best of my ability to help my family, friends, groups and the world."* ("Creed of the Church" and "Code of a Scientologist", both in [1].)

None of this is reflected by the CofS today. They have cast Hubbard in bronze and sell gold-leaf bound editions of his books and platinum-plated E-meters as "collectors items". A veritable hunting ground for the collector of relics! They have enshrined "the tech" and won't let anyone touch it. They don't dare go one step further than "what's written" – no matter how out-dated it may have become.

Hubbard found a set of axioms which he granted the importance of natural law. On the set theme of these axioms he improvised for the greater part of his life, finding ever-new solutions to the ever-changing problems presented to him by the cases of people. The great error being made by many scientologists inside and outside the CofS is that they mistake Hubbard's 30-year research for the ultimate in wisdom. Instead of following Hubbard's call and researching further – always and unvaryingly on the basis of the axioms – they elevate "what Ron says" to a dogma and introvert into solutions of the past. The implication of this is that while the majority have learned a lot about it, they believe they still have a long way to go before they manage – or dare to claim – to understand the subject. As it stands now, "the tech" in the CofS has lost its aliveness and became petrified. For those, however, who get gains from dancing around the monument of their godhead, it still serves a purpose.

Sectarianism

A MONOLITH CRUMBLES

As mentioned before: In 1983, immediately after the RTC was formed, hundreds and hundreds of old scientologists were declared suppressive persons. The majority of them had held high positions in the admin network or were experienced top auditors, often trained by Hubbard himself. A whole generation of scientologists who formed the living memory of Hubbard as a person, was wiped away within a few months without the application of any of the justice procedures they would have had a right to have. Some were kept for weeks in secret places in the California desert (Gilman Hot Springs, Happy Valley) under conditions similar to prison camps: men and women locked up together in toilets for days, beatings, chicanery.
As a consequence, many scientologists resigned from the CofS in protest. There was an actual mass walk-out – a phenomenon unbelievable even to those who themselves *did* the walking out.

It is hard to imagine for an outsider how deeply the lives of those who had suffered the 1982–83 purge were affected. A gigantic and vital stable datum had been taken away from people: the church was *not* a safe place; Ron was *not* infallible in his commandership. The question of whether scientology had only been applied wrongly or actually did not work (inconceivable so far) hung in the air like a big cloud of black smoke.
The CofS, unrelenting and self-righteous as always, issued a set of policies which cowed those who stayed into silence and made them denounce their best friends. The "outies" were ostracized. Disputes attempted by "outies" failed since "churchies" would simply turn their back. Those who didn't officially "disconnect" from their "outie" friends, were themselves excommunicated. "Disconnection letters", dictated to the "churchie" by his ethics officer, therefore were the order of the day.

To quote one as an actual example: "Hello John, I'm at London org getting some auditing. I'm totally not in agreement with what you are doing concerning scientology and I want you to stop it. I don't want to have any contact with you physically and mentally until you have handled your condition. – Paul."

Individually the effects of this often took on dramatic forms. Overnight the friends of yesterday didn't know each other when they met in the street; brothers wouldn't talk any longer with each other; mothers saw their sons leaving them and their daughters raging at them; business partners had actual walls put into their formerly common office space to separate their desks. Years, even decades of time, labour, efforts and hopes seemed wasted; private fortunes – in some cases hundreds of thousands of dollars – had gone up in smoke. And so some thousands went their way and closed a chapter on their life; some hundreds tried to congregate outside the CofS and find a new beginning; some dozens decided to pick up the E-meter and carried on. Around them, the lost and stray sheep began to gather. For most, this gregariousness was an unthinking action, an instinctive groping for the life-belt in a spiritual survival action. The lost group had to be replaced by a new group.

Getting the "outies" organised was first started in Los Angeles by former top tech man and International Case Supervisor, David Mayo, after he had been thrown out of the CofS as a "suppressive person". He started a network of "Advanced Ability Centers" (AACs) in the US and in Europe. After a promising start they collapsed because of the legal attacks from the CofS. Their reason: the "outies" had gotten hold of the confidential and well-guarded OT III materials and other OT levels. Suddenly there were not only those five Advanced Orgs of the CofS delivering the "secret" level of OT III, but some forty non-CofS centers throughout Europe, the US and Australia. Initially, in 1967, Hubbard imposed this secrecy because he considered that some aspects of the level could be profoundly disturbing and could even drive some individuals insane. However, to be realistic, it was more likely in 1983 that the CofS saw her hugely lucrative "mystery" threatened and her monopoly on it jeopardized. Either way, they attacked Mayo and some other leading staff of the AAC, by launching court cases against them. There was as well physical violence.

Mayo went down, yet the ball was kept rolling by a group forming separately in Europe under the leadership of William "Cptn.Bill" Robertson, Hubbard's right-hand man for sixteen years and top grade auditor. Robertson had the bulldozer-like intention to carry out what "the old man" had started (and what the CofS had studiously neglected to do), namely the galactic war against Xenu and his network by means of telepathic auditing techniques. He developed a refinement to the OT III technique, named it "Excalibur" (after a book Hubbard wrote in the 30's), trained a few dozen OTs on it who again trained others, and soon the intentions of many individual solo-auditors all around the planet once again started permeating Xenu's communication lines.

Thousands and thousands of solo hours were audited throughout the years of 1986 to 1988. The result: Xenu appeared no more. This being who had heavily interfered with individual sessions and been the contestant to hours-long telepathic wrestling matches, had disappeared from the scene. Auditors couldn't contact him any longer. Instead, lesser beings like lower executive staff of Xenu turned up – in control stations on far-away planets or in space ships orbiting Earth. They were no problem to audit and rehabilitate as soon as they learned that their master's game had come to an end.

A noteworthy side effect of Robertson's work were a whole load of data about the re-cultivation of Earth after the nuclear radiation from the incident 75 million years ago had ceased, and about the various galacto-political groups who were interested in shaping the future destiny of this planet – in a good as well as in a bad sense. In view of the data amassed by Robertson one may conclude that any cultural progress and any political catastrophe on Earth was brought about by "visitors from out there" – up to this day. As an example he interprets the tendencies towards a "One World Government", proclaimed since 1776, as a shrewd move to satisfy the colonial intentions from galactic confederations who have long since planned to add Earth to their empire. He regards the political inefficiency of Earth governments concerning the solution of the basic needs of man as a maneuvre to deceive people. By "playing the media", by well-aimed catastrophical news, by the arbitrary continuation of war, the population is to get the impression that the problems of this planet are too large to be solved by political means. In the face of the alleged desperateness of the situation man is to be driven to the point of reaching out *voluntarily* for the "helping hand from outer space" and empowering the rightful representative of our planet – the UNO – to take it. Which would make Earth a colony by plebiscit. Robertson summed up his thoughts in a manuscript called "Sector 9"; it is only privately circulated.

After Xenu was beaten, Robertson's group began to fall apart. In 1990, no organized followership of Hubbard outside the CofS has remained – at least none that would deserve mentioning. All in all, the independent auditors offer a fairly heterogeneous picture. Some are openly critical of Hubbard due to old personal grudges against him, some have gone off on a tangent of their own, due to their lack of comprehension of his work, some try to be "churchier" than the church itself in adhering to the letter of his words.

A "sect", according to the dictionary, is a "religious group separated from an established church". The word is derived from the Latin "secare", meaning "to cut off". Scientology as such is not a sect but a philosophy in its own right, with religious traits and based on a set of axioms. As long as Hubbard had the helm it was his personality which brought about what may be considered the "established church" of the definition above. Yet already *during* his "reign" side movements popped up in the wake of the CofS – be it because of personal rancor or a "know best" attitude. These are sects in the true sense of the definition.

Only after Hubbard's death did it become clear how low the spiritual cohesion of his movement actually was, how much it lived off a guiding personality. With that personality gone, all fell apart. Today, there are a good dozen sciento-logical sects. They congregate around the interpretation which their leaders give to Hubbard's work. As the CofS itself does not follow the intentions of Hubbard any longer and is far from comprehending the philosophical essentials of scientology, it is nothing but another sect – though admittedly the biggest.

THE PRAGMATIC VIEW

To make the picture look somewhat less gloomy it must be said that there are as well some auditors who look at scientology from a purely practical viewpoint. They take "the tech" – maybe for the first time ever – to the destination it was origi-nally designed for, and that is simply: *"the making of the individ-ual capable of living a better life in his own estimation and with his fellows, and the playing of a better game."* [15]

This form of therapy and personality development is the subject of this book. One might call it "pragmatic sciento-logy". It is not interested in the indoctrination of people or the forming of ideological brotherhoods. If anything went wrong with scientology, then it is its adherents' predelection for building strong images of leaders (Ron) and enemies (Xenu), and for forming conspiracy-minded groups around them. For those who are weak and in search for something to hold on to, for those who have never before read a book in their lives, scientology tends to become the thing of all things. They'll defend it and their group tooth and claw, i.e. the values, ideals and maxims they have uncritically absorbed, because their newly discovered spiritual survival depends on it. Small wonder that such groups finally turn fascist in character: it's due to the weakness of their members and the undisputed incomparability and infallibility of the leader.

This doesn't have to be so. It is indeed possible to adapt the methods of scientology to the needs of men and women and their problems and to help them in an acceptable fashion. Pragmatism instead of "superman-ism". It is indeed possible.

A "Cleared Planet" ?

When one, for a moment, forgets the unpleasant outgrowths of scientology in the form of ill-mannered groups and individuals and considers its purely spiritual value in the way its founder intended it, then Hubbard puts quite a claim there: *"A civilization without insanity, without criminals and without war, where the able can prosper and honest beings can have rights, and where Man is free to rise to greater heights, are the aims of Scientology."* [15]

This claim is not a new one. Many great men have attempted to achieve precisely this. And as soon as they voiced their claim, the opponents to it would get busy. It was always so. Any man who ever tried to get something done on this planet had a rough time, whether he was an artist, a philosopher, a scientist, a politician, a businessman or the founder of a spiritual movement which later turned into a new religion. And where did the tensions between the old and the new always manifest themselves the worst? Within the vicinity of the founder, of course, where the new impulse meets the old order which counters with infiltrators. Any Christ has his Judas. And so there was ingroup fighting and being right and making wrong and splintering off, but – on the whole – the idea couldn't be stopped. It survived in its pure form, its altered form, even in its opposites. Look at Buddha, Christ, Freud, Darwin, Galileo, Luther, Michelangelo, Einstein; look at how they were cursed and ridiculed at their time, and look at the schools of thought which followed in their wake. Even though these schools may have been trying to deny the truth of the work inspiring them – they still couldn't help granting it existence. And it always was time itself which in the end spelled out the value of the founder's thoughts and goals. The same will be the case with Hubbard and scientology.

The time coincidence between Hubbard's research and concurrent world developments deserve our attention. 1968 was the

73

year of student revolts across Europe, of the Russians taking Prague by tank power; it marks the peak of the Vietnam war and of the peoples of Earth feeling threatened by atomic warfare. Just then, Hubbard began to fight Xenu's powers by releasing OT III. Twenty years later, in 1988, Xenu ceases to show up in solo sessions. His power is broken. And a year later the Berlin wall falls, the USSR crumbles; again a year later (1990) the former archenemies USA and Russia join hands in the handling of world affairs. The cold war is over for good.

Whether these have anything to do with each other – this I leave up to you. You could argue that hell is still turned loose all around the planet; maybe worse than ever. I could counter that an outcry of protest is to be expected when a centuries-old suppression begins to lift off, and that the absence of the enforced stability one is accustomed to will lead invariably to chaos – until a new and self-determined stability has settled in. Apart from that a lot of work with individuals has to be done yet before there will be peace and quietness. Just because the general and his officers have taken to their heels, the troops do not know that the war is over and keep following their old orders. – But, as I said, whether these have anything to do with each other, that decision I leave up to the reader.

PART TWO:
The Principles Unveiled.

The "Technologies" of Scientology

INTRODUCTION

The philosophical part of this book covers the principle ideas of the theory of auditing. They may at first seem like a random collection of observations of human behaviour, but taken all together they form a structured view of how mental charge is the basis of life's problems, how it is generated, maintained, and how it affects an individual's life by giving rise to his "case".

Out of this view the procedures of auditing can be seen as an approach to guiding the pc progressively to discover and come to understand, the basis of his own charge and his effect on others, with consequent improvements in his "case".

The thirty-year growth of Hubbard's work can be seen as an attempt to evolve an integrated and generally workable conceptual system to describe and enhance human behaviour.

We are now going to look at the practical side of scientology, at its actual methods and their use in day-to-day life. We are going to look at its "technology" as Hubbard calls it. "Technology" simply means "a set of techniques". Much as one might use the word "methodology" instead, we are going to stick to "technology" or "tech" simply because there is a definite jargon within scientology which it is easier to adhere to than to break. Any jargon is useful as long as it makes sense and furthers the communication between practitioners, so we'll use it. "Scientologese" is quite a useful language once one has come to grips with it.

There are four technologies available in scientology: "study tech", i.e. the know-how of how to study for hours and hours with full comprehension and without fatigue; "admin tech", i.e. all things to do with organisation, management and production; "ethics tech", i.e. the leading of one's life by one's own integrity and honor; and "auditing tech". They all go back to the same philosophical foundations, formulated by Hubbard in the early 50's and called "The Factors", "The Axioms of Scientology", and "The Dianetics Axioms". All techniques used in scientology are derived from them, just as engineering techniques are derived from the natural law found by physicists. Hubbard did not "invent" the Axioms and the Factors; he only found and formulated them. He did invent "the tech", though. (Axioms and Factors will be referred to throughout Part Two.)

Of all the technologies mentioned we will mainly concentrate on auditing. Firstly, though, we are going to devote a few quick lines to the subject of study tech – for the benefit of the reader.

STUDY TECH

There are three barriers to study: the misunderstood word, the lack of mass, and the skipped gradient. All study problems can be reduced to these three barriers – given that the student is interested to start with, doesn't think he knows it all anyway, and studies on his own self-determinism. The "misunderstood word" is the most deceptive of the three. One reads through a paragraph, comes across a word one believes one understands and therefore does not look it up. Sooner or later one's concentration goes and the whole text doesn't seem to make sense any more.

The words one clearly identified as "not understood" or "half understood" are not the problem. These words one may easily go back to as soon as one loses track of the line of thought in one's text. Yet the word one always understood in *one* definition only, doesn't make sense when it is used in a *different* definition in the text. Not realizing this, one keeps on reading. Sooner or later one feels bored with the whole book and feels like throwing it against the wall. But one doesn't know which word it was! Because it didn't register as misunderstood when you were reading it.

So the rule is: when one feels bored or can no longer concentrate on a text one was previously interested in reading, one can be sure one passed a word one didn't fully understand. Remedy: one goes back to the place where reading was still fun and snoops around a bit. Sooner or later one will find a word one would have sworn one knew – but indeed, in this particular context it has a different meaning altogether. So one gets out a dictionary and clears the word in all its definitions, reads over the part after this word again and miraculously the text will be just as much fun as before. There will be no sign of boredom or lack of concentration.

Less deceptive but equally bothersome is the phenomenon called "lack of mass", the second barrier. "Mass" means as much as having a clear picture or the reality of the thing one is studying about. In order to have sufficient reality one must have been in physical contact with the thing and gained experience in handling it. One must have been in touch with the actual mass of the thing itself, with the material it's made of, it's size, weight, colour, way of behaviour etc.

When one is lacking this real-life experience with the thing one reads about, one naturally tries to imagine what it would be like. As one reads on one must keep on imagining and keep on imagining and keep on imagining until one finally feels all exhausted and weighed down by the pictures one made up in one's mind and the effort to keep them in place. Lacking the mass in front of one, one has become massy in the mind. This is the moment when one decides one "must take a break" because this subject is really "too difficult" and "wears one out".

Remedy: get a drawing, a picture, a film of the thing; better even: go out and find one to look at. If no such thing is available you can at least make a sketch or a graph of it, better even a clay model. You can also, valuably, push odds and ends around on the table to clarify the various interrelatednesses and mechanisms you are studying. The paperclips, marbles, bits of string become the objects in question, give the ideas more substance, get the images out of your head and hold them down in the real world.

The "skipped gradient" (third barrier) goes along with a feeling of confusion. It applies to activities rather than study of theory. One was learning a skill nicely step by step and felt very stable. Suddenly one feels confused, doubts one's ability to ever master it, feels uncertain and unhappy.

Remedy: go back to the point of certainty and see what step has been left out or would need to be put in to make it a smooth gradient. This of course depends very much on the degree of ability the student brought in to start with. Accordingly, his gradient has to be adjusted. Too low a gradient leads to boredom; too steep a gradient to confusion.

Here is an example: Joe wants to drive a car. He reads a book, becomes familiar with the main terminology, key words such as engine, steering wheel, clutch, chassis, wheels etc., until he has a general understanding of them. He understands the difference between a wheel and a steering wheel, and that a "chassis" doesn't serve to "chase" people, as the term may suggest. His understanding is a bit thin, though. It lacks substance. He may do some drawings to show how it works, and better still, plasticine models of the main parts, but seeing the real thing while studying is even more revealing. So he touches the wheels and feels the rubber and plays around with the clutch and accelerator pedals and follows the cables and pipes going in and out of the engine. Now he has the perfect balance between significance (the terms he studied) and mass (the actual car). – Driving, though, is a different story again. This is studying by doing, not by reading. And when the right teaching gradients are kept, Joe will turn out to be a capable and safe driver.

Simple as these things may look, they do straighten out the seeming complexities of study. Their remorseless application makes ladies perspire and strong men weep, but in the end it turns them into good students [17].

AUDITING

Auditing is not synonymous with "therapy", at least not in Hubbard's understanding of the word. With the exception of "Dianetics", he avoided the word "therapy" as he didn't mean his tech to be used in the same sense with medicine, psychiatry and psychology. This might generate the idea that his methods were applicable to the sick and disabled only. Of course, one does heal depressions, fears, compulsions and psychsomatic ills with auditing, yet the actual purpose of auditing would be better described in terms like "ability enhancement" or "personality development". The point is not to make an individual adapt to a "normality" prescribed by society, but to set him free to be, do and have whatever he desires.

Hubbard's concept of *"scientology – an applied philosophy designed and developed to make the able more able"* [2] implies that there is infinite expansion into ever new fields and dimensions of activity, that there is no standstill. It is a growth process, both in the spiritual and the material sense. And there is probably no person who wouldn't wish to grow in one or both of these aspects. Which is why auditing is for anyone and not limited to cases of psychosis and neurosis.

Looking at it from the outside, an auditing session appears not unlike a session in psychotherapy: two people in a room with the door shut, one asks and the other answers. Yet there are significant differences:

A session is not done by the clock but by end result. It is ended when a subject and the emotional charge connected with it have been worked through and when the pc has had a cognition about the state he was in which will enable him to initiate a change in his life. ("Charge", as we saw earlier, is mental tension as expressed by misemotion.) A session, accordingly, may last half an hour, three hours or even longer – in which case one takes breaks, of course.

Sessions are done as close to each other as feasible; there isn't just once or twice one hour per week. It is not unusual for a pc to run up 25 to 35 auditing hours within one week. This way a considerable discharge and relief is caused within a very short time. The pc will carry on living on a higher level of emotion and ability than when he came in, and, because he is winning now, his morale will be up, he'll carry on winning and won't easily fall into new depressions. The downward spiral has turned into an upward spiral.

Before a series of sessions is started, a thorough interview is done on the E-meter in order to detect all areas of charge the pc may have. Then an auditing program is developed by the auditor which considers the subjects the pc is interested in, brings them in their order of charged-ness (heaviest one first), and suggests one or more auditing processes for each one.

The auditor does not deviate from this program in session. He does not improvise. He stays flexible, yes, but only within the limits of the processes prescribed by the program. The quality and correctness of the program can be estimated by the amount of interest and gain the pc has. When he "goes out of session" (mentally speaking) the programm needs revising.

The auditor knows no more of the pc but what the pc has said about himself in the interview or finds out during the session. He "doesn't know all about him" just by looking at the way he sits in the chair. He is only interested in time, place, form and event of the incidents in the pc's past, and in the pc's considerations regarding them. The whole session is done by recall with the pc in his normal wakeful state. There are no drugs, hypnosis, electric shocks, trances, rites or initiation ceremonies. The pc will successfully re-experience his past traumata without any such aid. Once the original incident causing the pc's difficulties has been found and "run out", his psychosomatic or emotional troubles will disappear. As the auditor's task is to make the pc find the exact beginning of his troubles, and as these may be earlier than birth, it happens quite by itself that the pc slides into prenatal or even past life memories. This is not enforced by the auditor but a natural consequence of the pc's improvement in his recall ability and "confront" (i.e. mental stamina).

The auditor is bound to follow a code of behaviour, the "Auditor's Code". As the pc is aware of this code, he knows what he is to expect in the session. Amongst other things, the Auditor's Code demands that the auditor give no comments, opinions, evaluations, invalidations, or interpretations of any kind regarding the statements of the pc. He is not to do so either in or out of session, whether to the pc himself or any other person. As it is the auditor's task to help the pc find his own truth about himself and his life it is self-evident that he must not guide or "enlighten" him. The Auditor's Code is the mainstay of the trust the pc is setting in the auditor. It is a strictly functional code, the breaking of which would lead to immediate disaster [1].

The ultimate goal of an auditing cycle is the pc's ability to handle mental masses and energies all by himself, in which case he would be cause over his own mind, i.e. his imaginations, thoughts and pictures. This state is called "Clear".
From there on out, the pc would be fully responsible for himself and expand in life without further need of auditing. This result can only be attained by a number of intensive auditing cycles. If one were to only "fix up" a pc anytime life had knocked him about too hard, one would confirm his position on the effect side of things and not help him to be cause over them. In auditing one works towards an increase of responsibility and ability and is not satisfied with patch-up jobs.

In view of what is brought to light in sessions, the folk wisdom of "time heals all wounds" may be considered thoroughly disproven. The charge of an incident of 250 years ago is still there as soon as you put your finger on it. Those little bits of life energy tied up in the shock, pain and grief of that incident, are not recovered simply by time going by. They stay tied up. And each further bit of life energy tied up this way makes the person (thetan) shrink and wither – which is why children usually are more cheerful and enthusiastic than adults. The accumulation of failures and losses and the effort to keep them out of sight are a burden which increases from lifetime to lifetime. Life energy (theta) is locked up in all of this. After it has been regained, the person looks brighter, feels more hopeful, future-bound and active. This is the whole purpose of auditing.

The Laws and Mechanisms of Charge

This next section covers briefly the principle ideas of the theory of auditing. They may at first seem like a random collection of observations of human behaviour, but taken all together they form a structured view of how mental charge is the basis of life's problems, how it is generated, maintained, and how it affects an individual's life by giving rise to his "case". Out of this view the procedures of auditing can be seen as an approach to guiding the pc progressively to discover and come to understand, the basis of his own charge (and his effect on others), with consequent improvements in his "case".

The thirty-year growth of Hubbard's work can be seen as an attempt to evolve an integrated and generally workable conceptual system to describe human behaviour.

A FRUSTRATION SCALE

Charge, as we saw earlier, is mental tension one feels when things don't quite go the way they are supposed to. As long as one is certain about one's data, purpose or intention, one feels fine. The moment one becomes uncertain or doubtful one begins to feel nervous and uneasy. All of a sudden there is a "not-know". Before there was simply a "know". ("I know for sure that all birds fly. – Well, maybe they don't, actually . . . Most do, yes. But aren't there some which don't . . . ? I ought to look this up in a book.") The uncertainty created here is felt as mental strain (charge). It leads to curiosity and an attempt to find out. This, if not satisfied, will start a downward slide of frustrations. It goes along with a lowering of one's emotional tone.

Curiosity in itself is nothing bad. But still, it is charge in its finest form. Its satisfaction can be fun and rewarding. One feels it, for example, as one reads a crime story. One is thrilled by the mystery. One wants to find out "who's done it". Here we have a conscious "don't know/want to find out". This one might call "benevolent charge". It is the sort of tension without which an activity wouldn't be fun. There are enough odds to keep one entertained but not enough to make one feel a loser.

Now supposing there were a person, Mr. Roberts, who felt rather satisfied with crime stories and had the attitude of "I know what they are all about. You read a dozen and you know the rest of them." A good salesman could lure him out of this attitude and make him curious by saying: "Very well, sir, but you don't know *this* one. This one is special. There is nothing like it. You won't regret reading it." So Mr. Roberts might think: "Hm . . . maybe he is right. Maybe there is indeed a new idea on the market. Let's find out." And he buys the book.

The point of this story is that Mr. Roberts *created* the attitude of not-know. Surely, the salesman did his bit, too, but in the end it was Mr. Roberts who "un-knew" deliberately what he just knew for certain (which is that he is through with crime stories). He allowed himself to be drawn into the game of the salesman. It is Mr. Roberts' responsibility that he bought the book, and nobody else's. When the book turns out to be boring, Mr. Roberts will curse the salesman. But he can't deny that he himself decided that perhaps he *didn't* know all about crime stories. So he ought to put the blame on himself.

Here we have a trend from curiosity to aggressiveness, from "benevolent" to "malevolent" charge. Mr. Roberts thought this was no fun anymore. He felt cheated and was thoroughly annoyed. – We will investigate this downward trend in detail:

Mr. Roberts opens his newly-bought book at home and is *curious*. He reads a few pages and it isn't quite what he would have expected. But he *desires* to get something out of it and therefore carries on reading. It doesn't get better. Now Mr. Roberts *forces* himself to read on. He can't believe that this salesman should have sold just cheap rubbish to him. There *has* to be something good coming in this cursed story! Nothing coming, though. Mr. Roberts feels *inhibited* about reading on. It seems a waste of time, really. Doesn't improve his temper either. A few more paragraphs, and he puts it away. He *won't* read on. No good, this book. Didn't he know it in the first place? All crime stories are the same. He won't touch one ever again. Mr. Roberts *refuses* to have to do with the subject of crime stories in the future.

The difference between his initial attitude and that of now is an emotional one. To start with, he felt quite happy about not reading further crime stories. Now he feels an aggressive determination to not touch them again, ever !!

This development went along a scale. It goes "Know-Unknow-Curious-Desired-Enforced-Inhibited-No-Refused". It works with anything if you care to try it out. (It's called the CDEINR-Scale [1].)

Gradient scales are a tool often used by Hubbard to describe states and conditions. We will see more of them as we go on. The reason for them is that life is a flexible affair. There may be extremes, yes, but there are no absolutes, no "objective criteria". There is no absolute happiness or absolute sadness. These are relative terms – relative for each individual and therefore not comparable between individuals. Everybody knows for themselves when they feel more happy or more sad than the day before, or that they "feel happier than ever". It's *their* truth and not anyone else's truth. – Gradient scales, in the subjective world of the person's mind, measure a state only the individual can know to be true. (Reference: "The Logics" 6 and 7 in [1].)

REACH AND WITHDRAW

"Reach and withdraw are the two fundamentals in the action of theta", says Hubbard [2]. This follows from our story above. Mr. Roberts was reaching for the book, expressed as "curious-desired-enforced" on our scale. When his frustration rose and his hope of success dwindled, he withdrew from the book, expressed as "inhibited-no-refused".

Is there always reach and withdraw then, and no standstill ever? There can be standstill, too. Before Mr. Roberts participated in the game of the salesman he was in a state of knowing regarding crime stories. (Hubbard calls this **knowingness**, meaning "a state of being certain".) He felt perfectly happy and serene and relaxed about them. He had read his share and he had come to an endpoint and a conclusion about them and it had been a satisfying experience all in all. He felt neither reach nor withdraw. He was above any action with regard to the genre of crime stories. He was not *in* any action, he was *above* it.

There is yet another point of standstill: that *below* any action. When Mr. Roberts refused to have to do with crime stories ever again, he was not in the serene mood of before. He was upset. At this point a **ridge** was formed regarding crime stories because Mr. Roberts, in his anger, pushed mental energy against them. He resisted the inflow of further crime stories by developing a strong outflow against them. This ridge has a certain permanence. It will get activated anytime anyone dares to offer Mr. Roberts a crime story to read. Mr. Roberts is likely to react with no pleasure and without social graces. He will get outright angry.

This ridge, as it were, is "frozen theta". There is no flow; there is standstill. No reach and no withdraw. It's *below* the level of action. Action therefore is characterized by reach and withdraw. Above and below the level of action there is no reach and no withdraw. Charge, then, – to put it in very simple terms – is nothing but protest against something one doesn't like. When there is a stop to one's reach ("can't get there") or withdraw ("can't get away") one feels a protest; one feels charged up. This corresponds to the definition of **chronic charge**: *"the impulse to withdraw from that which can't be withdrawn from or to approach that which can't be approached and this, like a two-pole battery, generates current"* [2].

Referring back to Mr. Roberts: Let us assume he worked in a bookstore, exposed to whole shelves of detective stories. He is likely to feel extremely **restimulated**. Everytime he enters the shop in the morning his ridge starts cooking and keeps on cooking until he leaves in the evening. He feels like withdrawing from those shelves and can't as that would mean giving up his job. He feels like reaching for any other kind of book but can't because people keep ordering detective stories to be brought out to them. Constant protest, constant charge.

GAME THEORY

It has been mentioned before that the salesman managed to draw Mr. Roberts into his game. What is a game? *"A game consists of freedoms, barriers and purposes"* [2]. The salesman had the purpose to sell a book to Mr. Roberts. His barrier was Mr. Roberts' reluctance to buy one. His freedom consisted in the application of his persuasiveness. He had a game going. Mr. Roberts didn't, just then. Mr. Roberts had absolutely no games intentions regarding crime stories. So the salesman got Mr. Roberts involved in his game, and he won. He sold the book. Mr. Roberts lost. He went into the trap.

The three components mentioned above are all it takes to define a game. The absence of any of them means: no game. For example: Without a purpose one wouldn't even start a game. When there are either no barriers at all or unsurmountable barriers, there is no game either. No barriers means as much as total freedom. No opponent. No uncertainty about the outcome. Total predictability. This is not a game. It's tedious routine, at the most. Or it's a game played at the level of boredom. Unsurmountable barriers of course mean no freedom at all, no chance to win, full stop. No game. Between those two extremes, games are possible. Those games which provide a purpose, a proper balance between barriers and freedoms and therefore a chance to win, are regarded as fun.

Games tend to be taken seriously the more they concern the actual survival of a person. Such games tend to be played with a large amount of **self-determinism**. They must be won, no matter how. When chances are bad and it looks like the game was going to be lost, there usually is a considerable amount of effort put into the game: can't win but must win. The more one loses the more one goes into the game and keeps trying, keeps trying, keeps trying. One attempts to enforce success. There is a compulsive reach. When one has failed, has been beaten, has given up, there is a compulsive withdraw.

Should one manage to play it lightly, though, and not get all too serious about losing, one would contribute to the game as such no matter who wins. This is **pan-determinism**, the spirit of fair play.

When one only plays because one is told to or, worse, forced to, one has become an **other-determined** player. One plays on the determinism of others not one's own.

There are levels even below that: when one's will has been broken by violent means and one is made to carry on, one has become a **robot.** And below that there is a state of degradation where one is **oblivious** of the fact that one is human, a person, an individual. (See chapter K, section "Robotism", in [17].)

THE EMOTIONAL TONE SCALE

In the example of Mr. Roberts we could observe a lowering of emotion as his frustration increased. There is an exact scale connected to this which allows such unequivocal prediction that it compares to the natural laws of physics. It is the "emotional tone scale", a scale of moods. It was found as a result of auditing. Pc's can be observed to "come uptone" in a regular pattern. They first re-experience ("dramatize") the grief part of the engram, then show anger at the circumstances of the engram, then get bored talking about it, then show interest in certain details they never considered important before and finally end up in cheerfulness, laughing about the whole incident. They go "up the tone scale".

In or out of session, any person will follow this pattern, be it upwards or downwards on the scale. Sometimes it is done in leaps up or down, leaving out several tones in between, sometimes it goes tone by tone. But it is always along the same scale. In his book "Science of Survival", Hubbard deals extensively with it. [See 15, 16, 17, 18.]

Here are the major steps of the tone scale, going upwards: death wishes/apathy (0.0) – grief (0.5) – fear (1.0) – anger (1.5) – antagonism (2.0) – boredom (2.5) – interest (3.0) – cheerfulness (3.5) – enthusiasm (4.0). There are arbitrary numbers attached to them to make the intervals from tone to tone more graphically obvious. The steps shown here range from 0.0 to 4.0; the intervals are 0.5 in each case. To keep it simple, the in – between tones – of which there are many – are not shown [1, 2].

There is a little wisdom connected to this half-tone spacing: if you want to raise the emotion of your partner, just go half a tone above where he is and you'll see him come uptone. If you manage to keep the interval he'll finally end up being quite happy again. It's not *what* you talk about with him, it's *how* you say it. It's your tone level which counts. When you go down to his tone level, nothing changes except that there are *two* misemotional people now. When you are too high up compared to him you'll be unreal and he won't follow you up. – When you look at the times you successfully got someone uptone you'll probably find that you were applying this little wisdom without noticing. One can get pretty good at this. It takes some keen observation, though. (An auditor *must* know this scale by heart.) Language has many words to describe moods and feelings yet they all tie in with one or the other category of emotions on the tone scale.

So far, only the the middle part of the tone scale has been presented. It actually extends further upwards and downwards, from "serenity of beingness" (+ 40) to "total failure" (− 40). Along with the upper extreme go attributes like infinite space, infinite freedom, total absence of barriers, total knowingness. The opposite extreme at the bottom of the scale is characterized by infinite condensedness, no space, all barriers, no free-doms, unknow-ness. It is obvious that both extremes do not allow a game: there is no purpose in both cases, there are no barriers/all barriers, there is all freedom/null freedom. These conditions are called **no-game conditions**. The game called life happens between those two extremes.

(Most of human in-the-body experience is expressed within the 0.0 to 4.0 bracket. We won't look at the full scale here as it would go beyond the limits of this text.)

People simultaneously have two tones on this scale. One is the "social tone" which they try to keep up in order to make a good impression. Usually below that you find the "chronic tone", i.e. the genuine one. You can test a person for his chronic tone by startling him. He'll fall out of his "false pleasant-ness" (somewhere in the band of 3.0 = interest) and go right down into fear, for example – which is his real tone. You can tell by his face or by what he says. You can fully rely on this: a person will never drop lower than his chronic tone. He may take a dip further down if the news are too bad, but he'll soon settle on his chronic tone. After he has composed himself he will put his social tone back on.

The chronic tone is a sure indicator for the amount of engrams a person has in restimulation. The lower the chronic tone, the heavier his case weighs on the thetan. The **entur-bulated theta** (Hubbard's term) stirred up in the activated engrams works on him and pulls him downtone. His **free theta** creates the buoyancy which keeps him up. Antagonism (2.0) is the turning point on the scale. Above that there are positive emotions such as contentment and interest. From antagonism downwards **misemotion** begins. The person begins to be other-determined by his engram bank. A person who is chronically misemotional has a lot of engrams in resti-mulation (This explains why the auditor must keep a high level of interest throughout the session. One of the two people must be "above the bank" so that the other can discharge into him.)

The amount of free theta a person has at his disposal may expand or shrink, depending on the degree of restimulation he is suffering. His emotional tone is a direct expression of the proportion between free theta and enturbulated theta.

There is another indicator yet for this proportion: the person's fluidity or fixity of **attention**. Free theta and free attention are two terms describing the same thing. The more free theta she has the more she can direct her attention by her own volition. As she sinks on the scale (because she fought too many barriers unsuccessfully), her free theta diminishes and her attention becomes compulsively fixed. In antagonism and anger, she would use her attention like an explosive to blast the opponent out of her space; in fear, her attention would be fixated on the opponent as if by rivets. In apathy none is left; her gaze would wander aimlessly about.

THE ARC TRIANGLE

We have used the term "theta" already a few times now. What exactly *is* theta? Where does this "life force" come from? Is it just there like the air one breathes? Or is it made somewhere? In order to clarify this question properly we will have to refer to the very foundations upon which Hubbard's philosophical structure rests: the Scientology Axioms and the Dianetic Axioms. They will be quickly introduced before we go on. (There is a third set, the Factors, which won't concern us as yet. They'll appear in a later section.)

As the word has come up, we'll have to define it. What are axioms, be it in scientology or in physics? They are laws, principles and agreements so fundamental that they cannot be argued about. They can neither be proven nor disproven. All logical deductions start from there. If one could think "further down" than them, they wouldn't be axioms.

Hubbard presented the *Dianetic* Axioms in 1951. They cover the complete spectrum of scientology thought but put specific emphasis on the organism. They look at life not so much from the viewpoint of the thetan running the organism but from the organism itself. There are 194 of them. The *Scientology* Axioms were issued in 1954. They cover the same spectrum as the Dianetic Axioms but emphasize the viewpoint of the thetan. As a thetan is less complex in his actions than an organism, the Scientology Axioms are much more condensed than the Dianetics Axioms and therefore number only 58. (Dianetics Axioms, when referred to, will be abbreviated to "Dn Ax."; Scientology Axioms to "Ax.". For references see [1].)

All auditing processes and methods of dianetics and scientology go straight back to the Axioms. Anything not aligned with the Axioms won't work. This is not only true for scientology techniques but as well for any other technique addressing the spirit, be it meditation, psychotherapy or the rites of medicine men. This is quite a claim, I know. But it's true. At least I found it so.

Let us now return to the question posed. What is theta, really? *"Theta is an energy existing separate and distinct from the physical universe"* [2].

Theta and thought, in Hubbard's terms, are synonymous: *"Thought is considered as a kind of "energy" which is **not** part of the physical universe. It controls energy, but has no wavelength. It uses matter but has no mass. It is found in space but it has no position. It records time but it is not subject to time"* [2].

The reasoning behind this statement is: theta is "life force" or "thought power". It animates the organism. Therefore it must be senior to the organism. *"An organism without thought is already dead"* [2]. Since an organism is part of the physical universe it follows that theta (thought) cannot as well be part of the physical universe. Theta works on the physical universe from outside it. Thought, or theta, does not move but makes things move. Itself it is **static**; the action it causes is **dynamic**. (See Dn Ax. 1–5.)

Now that we know what theta is defined as, the question remains where and how it is made. To answer this, one must know what theta consists of: *"The component parts of theta are affinity, reality, and communication"* (Dn Ax. 110). The same is true for understanding: *"Understanding is composed of affinity, reality and communication"* (Ax. 21).

"Theta" and "understanding" apparently are synonymous. This is easily demonstrated. Anytime one feels understood by another one's free theta increases and one goes up the tonescale. Increasing understanding and increasing theta amount to the same: a rise on the tonescale.

In order to *feel understood* one must have been listened to (communication); one must have received a sign from one's partner to show that he got what one meant to say (reality); one must feel comfortable with him and well-liked (affinity). After such a conversation one feels relieved. Maybe one came uptone from grief to anger regarding the affair one felt troubled by. (Quite an improvement!) – In order to *increase theta* one usually does "something nice". One has had terrible trouble in the office and is all upset on the way home. How does one get one's tone up: by taking a walk. One communicates with trees and plants, feels in agreement with them and appreciates them. One has increased one's ARC. Result: the annoyance at the office has lost its sting; it has become boring and unimportant.

Conclusion: one does not have to be in touch with a person necessarily in order to regain one's balance. How one builds up theta is of no importance. There are many possibilities. As long as there is an increase in communication, reality and affinity, one will eventually feel better.

An understanding person could be described as "thetaful". She has a lot of love to give, a lot of free theta to spend, a lot of spare attention for everyone. Such a person will not have much trouble in life. She may never be terribly successful in terms of rank and status, yet she will be well liked and have great peace of mind. This quality was not given to her as a birthright. It is something she creates causatively by using affinity, reality and communication.

"Affinity, reality and communication co-exist in an inextricable rela-
tionship. (. . .) None can be increased without increasing the other
two and none can be decreased without decreasing the other two"
(Dn Ax. 168). They stand with each other in a triangular rela-
tion. There are always the three of them there and influencing
each other, no matter which one you work on. You talk to
someone about the weather (comm), you come to an agreement that this summer isn't really worth remembering (reality), you begin to think he's a great old chap (affinity). Or: You
ask your neighbour's son who is a little shy usually, about his
new bike (reality). He'll bubble over with pride and excite-
ment about it (comm). You tell him you wished you had had a
bike like that when you were his age (agreement/reality). He'll
like you better from now on and be less shy (affinity). Or: you
pat a dog (affinity). He'll leap up and bark at you playfully
(comm). You pick up the idea from him and take him for a
walk (reality).

This, then, is the "ARC triangle". By increasing or decreasing
ARC you can boost or reduce understanding. It all depends on
your intentions. ARC, understanding and theta all mean the
same, as it turns out. They don't exist without the thetan. It follows that the thetan himself produces the theta he works with.

Going back to the tone scale for a moment: now that we know
the concept of ARC we can easily recognize that the tone scale
measures the ARC of a person. Before, we said it measures
the proportion between free theta and enturbulated theta.
Now we say that it measures the person's potential of understanding. It's the same thing. Example: try talking to an angry
man. He won't understand. He has little free theta; his capa-
city for understanding is comparatively low. If he were in fear,
it would be even lower. In antagonism, he'd get it but throw it
back at you. Up in boredom he'd get it and keep it without doing anything with it. And so on up the scale.

Let us now look at the definitions of A and R and C separately
and add some of the philosophical depth needed later on in
our discussion.

AFFINITY

Hubbard defines **affinity** in terms of reaching. One reaches for something in order to have it close to one. Lack of affinity would be expressed in a withdraw. *"Affinity is a phenomenon of space in that it expresses the willingness to occupy the same place as the thing which is loved or liked. The reverse of it would be antipathy (. . .) which would be the unwillingness to occupy the same space as or the unwillingness to approach something or someone"* [2].

It follows that the "mental space" of someone widens with the amount of things or people he loves. It follows as well that someone high on the tonescale, having a lot of affinity, has no problem with including a lot of things or people in his space. He manages to look at life from other viewpoints as well as his own. That's a true sign of affinity. He is able "to put himself in someone else's shoes" and look at things from their angle.

Put in more technical terms: he can assume the **beingness** of another, his role, his identity. This doesn't refer to people only but to all things alive or dead, such as plants and stones. Given enough affinity, one can deliberately "become them". This is so because the thetan is not part of the physical universe but places himself in the physical universe wherever he considers it useful or pleasant to be (Ax. 44, 45). Usually one has one's viewpoint stably anchored inside one's head. Yet simultaneously one may put a viewpoint into a withering plant on the windowsill, and "wander around inside it" to find out what's wrong with it. One has, for a moment, assumed the beingness of this plant. *"Coincidence of location and beingness, that is the ultimate in affinity"* [2]. There are many ways to assume a beingness, to be in the space of another or make another be in one's space. There is (once again) a whole scale to it, parallelling the tone scale: the "Know-to-Mystery Scale". (*All* scales parallel the tone scale!)

Assuming the beingness of another may be done by knowing, by looking, by emotional tuning-in. Beingness can be assumed by effort, by intellectual figuring, in symbolic form, by eating, sex or mystery rites. Examples: An artist gets into the spirit of things and expresses it by dance, painting or music; a hunter shoots his lion to share the same space with him; a cannibal eats his victim's brains to assume his beingness; sex orgies serve to be "close to each other" – at least physically. The further you get down on this scale the more solid the means become to attain the end of assuming someone's beingness. Instead of theta, mest is used (Ax. 25).

REALITY

Reality is not looked at as "objective" by Hubbard. It is certainly observable, yet not necessarily objective. Each observer takes his own viewpoint, in both senses of the word: a) Mentally speaking, he sees things through the filter of his own attitudes and considerations, and with the amount of affinity he happens to have at the time. (Someone all sad and griefy makes a bad observer.) b) Physically speaking, each observer stands in a different location from the other and therefore has a different angle of view. Therefore each observation, to start with, exists for each observer individually only. It is actually in his mind. This is termed an **actuality**. As soon as the observers share their observation and come to an agreement with each other, there is "reality" in the full sense of the word: *"An actuality can exist for one individually, but when it is agreed with by others it can then said to be a reality"* (Ax. 27).

This does not exclude that one might disagree with oneself occasionally. Off and on "one doesn't trust one's own eyes", as we all know. So even for oneself one sometimes has to work out what is real and what isn't. Reality changes can easily be induced by drugs and hypnosis, even by mere physical threats and violence. You can beat somebody's own reality out of him and make him agree to yours. He'll do it because he wants to live. This way robots are made.
In any case, when we talk about reality, we talk about agreement. *"Reality is the agreement upon perceptions and data in the*

physical universe. (All we can be sure is real is that on which we have agreed is real. Agreement is the essence of reality.)" (Dn Ax. 113)
But: just because a few people have agreed on something does not necessarily mean that it is "truly so". By whose standards anyway? Ask some other people and you'are bound to find a different agreement on the same matter. Reality is therefore *"the agreed-upon apparency of existence"* (Ax. 26). It's only an apparency. It may look solid one day; it may change the next day. You never can tell. Even our scientific description of the physical universe is only *one* way of coming to an agreement concerning it. Cross-cultural studies (particularly in the field of medicine) show that other agreements are possible and when acted upon, bring results, too.

COMMUNICATION

"Communication is the interchange of perception through the material universe between organisms or the perception of the material universe by sense channels" (Dn Ax. 114).
Simply put: just by perceiving something one is already involved with communication and – thereby – with the ARC-triangle. The perception is real or not to the extent that one can agree with it or not. Perceptions which one can agree with to some extent and which happen to fall into line with one's survival efforts, one has affinity with. Others which may be off one's line of survival or go against it, one may grudgingly accept as real but one surely doesn't like them. When too rough, one may not even perceive them at all: no communication, apathy (Dn Ax. 113).

The term "interchange" in the quotation above implies that there are two terminals involved in a cycle of communication. "Terminal", originally a computer term, means in scientologese "the end of a communication line". There are two: source-point and receipt-point. Thus the definition of communication looks like this:

"Communication is the consideration and action of impelling an impulse or particle from source-point across a distance to receipt-point, with the intention of bringing into being at the receipt-point a duplication and understanding of that which emanated from the source-point" (Ax. 28).

Duplication means: taking in the exact reality of the thing, seeing it as it is without any distortions, without adding to or subtracting from it. Duplication refers to the communication-part of the ARC triangle. A perfect duplication of the particle received would be the optimum end of the actual action of communication.

Understanding means: a) comparing the data received with data already known so that they make sense. That's the reality-part. (See Logics 8-12; in [1].) b) Developing an emotional attitude; liking or disliking the message or its sender. That's the affinity-part.

From the definition above the **communication formula** is derived: *"Cause, distance, effect, with intention, attention, duplication and understanding"* [2]. It's a formula in the dictionary sense of "recipe or prescription". When you mix the ingredients in the formula you get communication. If you leave one ingredient out, it won't be communication.

With the above, one important aspect of an auditing session has been described: the preclear makes himself receipt point of the energy impulses and mass particles which emanate from the ridge or engram. He duplicates and understands them one by one until all informations contained in the picture have been fully included in his space. Now the picture will vanish. It won't be a compulsive inflow on the pc any longer. If he wants to, he can re-create it at will. But there won't be any *compulsive* re-creation of it.

Observing the ARC triangle in session, one usually finds the pc works with it in reverse order because communication is "the easy way in". This is how it goes: 1. The pc goes in communication with the thing (engram, ridge, picture) by permitting himself to perceive it. 2. He duplicates its reality until he can agree with the thing being this way and no other. 3. He admires it (gives it affinity) for being the way it is instead of resisting it – at which moment its power over him will vanish.

As the pc progresses through his sessions he regains more and more free theta and therefore comes uptone. In the end he will be strong enough to work with affinity only. He sees the picture, permeates it with his affinity and instantly picks up its reality. No drawn-out laborious communication needed, no looking at it this way and that way until finally the whole thing can be confronted. No, it's one glance and the picture goes up in smoke. This is called "blowing by inspection" (auditor jargon). It means that the pc won't have a long way to go anymore before he is Clear.

CONFRONTING

There was a word in the last few lines of the section above which deserves our special attention. It is the word "confronting". Hubbard uses it in its dictionary sense with particular emphasis on "not flinching, keeping cool". Confronting is *the ability to be there comfortably and perceive*[2]. It means calmly holding one's position without either reaching or withdrawing. It means being there, comfortably, and seeing something as it is. It is a state of being, not of doing. Doing follows from it later.

Consequently, "good confront" is the one and only prerequisite to exact duplication. A man in panic won't see any more what's right in front of his nose. He does not duplicate. Duplication therefore is the prerequisite to understanding, full ARC and a high position on the tone scale.

Three interesting maxims may be derived from this:

"The degree of complexity is proportional to the degree of non-confront.

The degree of simplicity is proportional to the degree of confront.

The basis of aberration is a non-confront." (HCO PL 18 Sept 1967)

If you were interested in making life complicated, here is a sure way: do not confront it.

When we combine the data about ARC, tonescale and confronting, we get a "Scale of Confront" [1]. It may be observed in anyone recalling anything, in or out of session. Its lowest stage is characterized by the pc putting something else there than what's really there. (This is called "dub-in".) Above that there is seeing blackness or absolutely nothing. Further up follows the effort to mentally "be elsewhere" as a solution to confronting. (You find that in people who complain about "nervousness" or "lack of concentration" as an excuse for not doing their job properly.) Above that is the actual ability to confront. Next step up: the willingness to experience what goes on in the situation, in the other person or in the engram, and to participate in what goes on. And the final step: assuming the beingness of it, identifying with it knowingly and at will, looking at life from the other viewpoint. The top of the tonescale merges with the top of the confront scale. Result: charge blown or situation handled, respectively. (All scales merge at the top, by the way.)

POSTULATES AND CONSIDERATIONS

In the section on games, the word "purpose" was used. There is another word for it, very much a "scientology" tech word. It is **postulate.** Postulate means: one is putting something there as true. It is a truth one has created for oneself and by oneself, and it may be true for oneself alone. It is a *"self-created truth"* [2].

Postulates may refer to the present, past or future. Take Mr. Jones, for example. He says: "Next weekend I'll be out fishing." When he says it it's true for him. With this statement he has created his *future.* If you were asking Mr. Jones for his name and his trade, you'd get a postulate referring to Mr. Jones' *present* as an answer. He'll say: "My name is Jones and

I am a farmer". This may sound blatantly obvious and not worth mentioning in the context of postulates; nevertheless, it is something Mr. Jones considers very true for himself. (Postulates which aren't a one-off thing but are continuously held up, are termed **considerations**.)

You may think it should be difficult to shake Mr. Jones' certainty about his name and about his being a farmer, yet it can be done with the classic brainwashing and implanting methods of electric shocks, drugs and hypnosis [8]. A comparable effect may be brought about by Mr. Jones becoming reactively identified with the content of an engram, particularly with one of the "dramatis personae" in the engram. As a result of this identification he walks around thinking he is Napoleon. Mind you, he is not recalling having been Napoleon. He thinks he is Napoleon *now.* This certainly is a postulate determining his present, if only an **aberrated** (insane) one and imposed on him by the engram.

Mr. Jones has postulates about his *past* too. One of them is: "My father is William Jones." Mr. Jones believes this to be true. One day he is told by someone that his father died when his mother was three months pregnant, that his mother re-married when he was five months old and that his real (physical) father's name is Stephen Francis. This may come as quite a shock to Mr. Jones since it would break a consideration he has upheld for a very long time.

Evidently, man creates his past, present and future by postulates. His past, present and future exist to the extent that he can postulate them. A man in low spirits has a dim future or even none at all. A hightoned person postulates a splendid future for himself and makes it happen. Someone in apathy never washes his dishes or cleans his room because "it's too much work" or "there is no time for this"; a cheerful person does it in five minutes. And so on. *"Space, energy, objects, form and time are the result of considerations (. . .)"* (Ax. 3).

103

THE CYCLE OF ACTION

Conclusion from the previous section: What is true for oneself – whether referring to the past or the future – is true *now*, simply because postulates are always now, once they have been made. This is because postulates are **thoughts**. They are thoughts connected with action or states of being, so they have a dynamic connotation, but still: they are thoughts. And thoughts, as we saw, exist outside the physical universe. The physical universe – or "mest universe" – consists of the components matter, energy, space and time (mest). Thought is outside and above time and therefore outside and above the mest universe. Thoughts and postulates impinge on the physical universe to give it shape, form and dynamic action, yes, but they are not part of it. Thoughts and postulates all by themselves are static. They don't move, they are not dynamic, yet bring about dynamic action. They "float along in time" as it were; they are always in the present, forever now, no matter when they were made. The totality of all postulates ever made are expressed in the Now of each moment. They determine life in each instant.

How does one undo a postulate then? There is only one way: one must duplicate it exactly as it was made originally; one must recreate it 100% exact in a new unit of time. Then it will be cancelled. If one is only a fraction off, it will stay. Example: you made a postulate 1500 years ago that life wasn't worth living unless you had seen a live unicorn. It didn't work out that lifetime. Next lifetime you sort of forgot about the actual postulate but you kept catching yourself thinking of unicorns off and on, and wondered why. It went on like this for 1500 years up to the present lifetime. Today you are a great collector of books and learned essays about unicorns. You know it's all fantasy and you have an educated scientific viewpoint on it and you consider it just a quaint little hobby, but – and here is the point – you don't know how come you should be so fascinated with unicorns. The postulate keeps going. And it will keep on going until you realize with a flash (in or out of session) that "life isn't worth living as long as I haven't seen a live unicorn". Not only must you realize this, but you as well must take this realization seriously and accept it, instead of pushing it aside as "part of my stupid unicorn-madness".

With this realization you have made the perfect duplicate of the original postulate, and you made it in a new unit of time. You made it as if you were making it now and had never made it before. It's not: "I seem to recall that some long time ago I had this thing about unicorns and it appears to have stuck with me. Guess I'll drop the habit now." Oh no. This won't work. It has to be done now as if it had never occured to you before, and it has to be the exact same thought. With this done your compulsive interest in unicorns will vanish. (Ax. 12, 15, 16, 20.)

There is another possibility to end this story: one morning you walk in the park and there's a unicorn right there on the lawn; a live unicorn, right there! You can hardly believe your eyes, but it's there. You look at it and it looks at you, and then it walks away. After this experience you feel a tremendous sensation of fulfillment, calmness and serenity. A wish of 1500 years ago finally come true! What relief. – In this case the perfect duplicate was in real life. And that's one other way to end a cycle of action.

From this chain of thoughts the concept of the **actual cycle of action** is derived. It starts with creating a postulate and then creating life on the basis of this postulate. And it goes on creating-creating-creating and never stops, until the original postulate is un-created by means of a perfect duplicate. The cycle of action does not come to an end by counter-creating. That only gives you a ridge. Counter-creating doesn't do away with the postulate. When you get sick and tired of your unicorn fanatism and throw all your books about unicorns in the rubbish bin, you still haven't cancelled your postulate. You have worked against it, suppressed it, invalidated it, yes, and you made a nice fat ridge this way. But you didn't cancel the postulate because you didn't make a perfect duplicate (Ax. 17, 18).

In the physical universe, there is a seemingly different cycle of action. It goes create – survive (or persist) – destroy. At least, that's the way it looks like from the outside. Beneath this **apparent cycle of action**, though, one again finds postulates. Example: there is this village church, 350 years old, lightning strikes, it burns down. It was created, persisted through time, and was destroyed. End of cycle? No. There is a huge agreement amongst the villagers that they can't do without their church. So they collect money and rebuild their church exactly as it was. You can't tell it's a re-make when you walk past it. (Actual example.)

And this church may burn down again, and they'll for sure build another one. Any style would serve, as long as they have their church. And they will keep doing so no matter how often their church burns down until they will finally have a cognition on the reason they wanted to have a church in the first place. And then they may reconsider and not build another one. But this group cognition is not likely to occur as it would take getting together everybody who ever helped postulating this church into existence, each builder, priest, baptized child, married couple, deceased citizen laying in state, or photo-happy tourist.

Of course, not everything which was destroyed is built up again. There are many reasons. One way of terminating a group postulate is by the group ceasing to exist. Let's say our village were becoming populated to a large percentage by city people, with the locals slowly dying out. There would be no-one left to keep up the original church-postulate. Lacking intention as its driving force, the postulate would gradually peter out. Which does not mean that it was cancelled; it just became drowned in apathy. (The passing stage on the way there is nostalgia – 0.5 on the tonescale: grief.) It could be easily revived if enough people were actively backing it up.

One reason for not re-building the church may be lack of money. But that doesn't kill off the intention behind it, provided

106

the villagers were still backing up the idea. It would only temporarily stall the realization of the project. (Ax. 13, 14.)

To summarize, this idea of "cycle of action" is a way of looking how creation occurs. In the shared physical world things are brought into being because of postulates, and then because of the interaction of the myriad other influences, such as other people's postulates, they may change, decay, or be destroyed. There is an interaction of many continuous create-create-create cycles of all the contributors with their conflicting purposes. So the actual cycle of action is the subjective one, and the cycle of action that occurs in the "real" world is only an apparency. (This would hold true down to the existence of the universe itself if one assumed, as Hubbard did, that its reality is only an agreement between all the participating thetans, that life, spirit, theta is senior to mest.)

From the two different cycles of action two different concepts of time may be derived. The actual cycle of action measures "subjective time" in the form of a sequence of complete cycles of action. The apparent cycle of action measures the "objective time" which has been agreed upon: sunrise-to-sunset, moon phases, the hands moving on the clock dial.

Both types of time are covered by the Axioms 7, 8 and 9: *"Time is basically a postulate that space and particles will persist. The apparency of time is the change of position of particles in space. Change is the primary manifestation of time."*

GOALS PROBLEMS MASSES (GPMs)

There is a specific terminology which goes with the "actual cycle of action". It describes the various states or conditions the individual undergoes in this sequence of "create, create-create-create, uncreate or, conversely, countercreate". Counter-creation, as we have seen, doesn't undo the original creation and complete the cycle of action. It only forms a ridge called a **GPM** or **Goals Problems Mass**. It is a mass which was formed because one couldn't handle the problems connected with one's goal, and gave up. A GPM and a ridge are the same, really, except that the term "GPM" describes the formative process of a ridge, whereas the word "ridge" itself refers to the end product. An engram is a ridge, too. The difference between engram and GPM is that the engram is a recording by the body of what happened to the body, whereas the GPM contains data on what happened to the thetan himself.

To exemplify the formation of a GPM, let us regard the life of Gopdhal Khan, an immensely rich and famous 17th century Moghul prince who ruled over Persia at that time. Two versions of his life story have been passed down to posterity, one with a happy end and the other with an unhappy end. We'll take the happy-end one to start with.

Gopdhal Khan was a man who loved the arts. As well he was a man who lived in a rather modest palace – too modest to accommodate all the private and political activities of court life. One day it happened – when Gopdhal Khan looked at his palace from a distance and saw it for the shabby place it was – that he, quick as lightning, had a vision of something undescribably splendid and beautiful superimposed on the old palace, and he knew with innermost certainty: "I'm going to build the house of my dreams". He didn't have any picture of it, nothing concrete and definite. A pure postulate. And he knew he was going to do it.

This condition of knowingness which exists at the moment of creation of a thought, is termed an **as-isness** (Ax. 11). It contains no time as it stays forever with the person who made it. It is always *now*. Neither does it contain matter, energy or space, or any picture. Postulates, as we saw before, are outside mest. This is true for physical as well as mental mest, i.e. for pictures. The state of as-isness is the moment one conceives the thought or postulate exactly as it is, the pure unadorned and un-camouflaged postulate.

Gopdhal Khan went and told his master builder about it. He told him all the purposes connected with this palace and all the guidelines that were to be kept to ensure the perfect outcome. Together they worked out the "ideal scene" [19]. The builder made some sketches and drawings and in the end he made a large plaster model of the palace-to-be, all painted and adorned, with gold roofs and marble gates. Then the construction of the actual palace started. Four years later it was finished. Gopdhal Khan beheld it, tears of joy came to his eyes and he said: "This is it! This is the house of my dreams!" – He moved in and there was not a single day for the rest of his life that he did not feel a sense of joy and fulfillment because of his palace.

Three things have happened here. Firstly, the static postulate was pulled down to the level of dynamic mest action (mental as well as physical) and worked upon. Secondly, the final product, i.e. the "existing scene" [19] of the newly-built palace, totally matched the ideal scene, which again matched the actual postulate. A perfect duplicate of it had been created in the mest universe. Thirdly, when Gopdhal Khan said that this was it, this *was* the house of his dreams, he fully acknowledged the postulate as having come true. Thereby the postulate vanished. It had been fulfilled. The cycle of action had come to its end. A second as-isness occurred here, marking the moment of destruction of the postulate. An as-isness, therefore, *"is the condition of existence which exists at the moment of creation and the moment of destruction"* (Ax. 11).

This is the happy-ending story of Gopdhal Khan and his palace. Let us turn to the unhappy version. What occurred? Well, the story developed as above up to the point when the construction of the actual palace was started. After a year and a half, with everything progressing satisfactorily, Gopdhal Khan went to see his cousin, the prince of Radjastan, on a social visit. It took a year. When he came back, he learned that the enemy had been in the country. He saw his old palace destroyed, his new palace destroyed, the builder killed and all the plans and models burnt. He sat down, wept, and thought: "You never get what you want".

And so he made a second postulate altering the first one. (The first one was: "I'll built the house of my dreams".) Yet a second postulate does not cancel the first one; it only alters it. Both co-existed from now on in Gopdhal Khan's mind. This condition of existence is called **alter-isness** (Ax. 11).

In the years to come, Gopdhal Khan made it go right as much as he could to fulfill his obligations as a ruler. He had a new palace built without caring too much what it looked like. He somehow settled in on the reality of the situation. He said to himself: "Well, I'm actually quite all right this way. I have a roof over my head and the country is in good shape". – This condition of existence is called an **is-ness**. An is-ness is the result of an alter-isness. It is an agreement with what is, after giving up on what should be (Ax. 11).

Yet Gopdhal Khan never really recovered from the blow. He sighed a lot when he thought of his beloved palace, and turned bitter. The is-ness of his life could not make him forget his dreams. He took to smoking hasheesh for comfort and spent the rest of his days in clouded oblivion. – This final condition of existence is called a **not-isness** (Ax. 11).

"Ax.18: The static (i.e. thetan), *in practicing not-isness, brings about the persistence of unwanted existences, and so brings about unreality, which includes forgetfulness, unconsciousness, and other undesirable states."*(Note: The words "static" and "thetan" actually mean the same. They are often used interchangeably by Hubbard. Sometimes their use depends on the aspect to be emphasized: that of the player in the game – the thetan, or that of the one "above the games" – the static.)

Gopdhal Khan's trouble really started with him making a second postulate ("can't have") meant to mask the first one ("want to have") in such a way as to pretend that the first one wasn't really there any more. He tried to make himself forget as the obstacles seemed unsurmountable: he was getting old, his builder was dead, his private fortune had been robbed by the enemy. The dream palace game had come to an end, obviously. It was only realistic to say so. You never get what you want, just shows you. This second postulate of "you never get what you want", will continue eternally along with the first one. It's a pair of postulates. This is what a GPM really is: a pair of postulates or intentions of comparable magnitude, locked up with each other. Whenever he thinks of one, he has to think of the other. So it's best not to think of either. That's where hasheesh helps.

What has been built here, is a battery of ever-lasting inexhaustible potential. Postulates are eternal. GPMs, consisting of two interlocked postulates, are eternal, too. All that has to happen is the restimulation of one of them and the other will spring to mind, and charge and mass and misemotion will result.

To put it bluntly: Gopdhal Khan has lied to himself. Yes, it was "realistic" to say that in view of circumstances the palace game was over. But this realism is nothing but the expression of an agreement with an alter-isness. At the bottom of his heart Gopdhal Khan knew that he wanted his dream palace and never had stopped wanting it. And obviously, the alter-isness did not end the problem – it actually started and persisted it! Had Gopdhal Khan rolled up his sleeves, spat on is hands and said: "All right people, we may not get there all the way, but we can at least try", he would have lived by the truth he knew, i.e. without any alter-isness.

"Ax 38: 1. Truth is the exact consideration. 2. Truth is the exact time, place, form and event. (. . .) we can achieve a persistence only when we mask the truth. Lying is an alteration of time, place, event, or form. Lying becomes alter-isness, becomes stupidity. Anything which persists must avoid as-isness. Thus, anything, to persist, must contain a lie." "Ax.36: A lie is a second postulate, statement or condition, designed to mask a primary postulate which is permitted to remain." "Ax.37: When a primary consideration is altered but still exists, persistence is achieved for the altering consideration." "Ax.33: Any as-isness which is altered by not-isness (by force) tends to persist."

Now supposing Gopdhal Khan had kept on working to get his palace built. But, what with his reduced means and his master builder dead, he still hadn't got what he wanted. On his death

111

bed he might have said: "Well, I tried up to the last minute, but you can't expect to get what you want". So what help is that? The same second postulate, the same alter-isness, just made later!

The biggest lie here is the "one-lifetime-consideration" as Hubbard calls it. Saying things like that on your deathbed means you believe you *are* a body and not an immortal spirit who can *use* bodies until he gets what he wants. Supposing a Buddhist monk had come along to sit at Gopdhal Khan's death bed and said to him: "Look, I have news for you. There is a next life." Certainly Gophal would have said: "Is that so? Oh great! Then I can try to get my palace next lifetime. All it takes is finding a good body in the royal family. Which reminds me: my daughter-in-law is pregnant. I'd better die fast!" And off he goes.

Which shows how to undo a GPM: just take the second postulate (the alter-isness, the "can't have") away and the thetan is going full steam again on the first one (the as-isness, the "want to have").

MENTAL MATTER,
ENERGY, SPACE AND TIME

So far we have covered how charge is generated and how it can be undone. One aspect remains to be looked at: that of restimulation. To clarify this we need yet another set of concepts. We'll go through them and then return to the subject of restimulation.

Hubbard defines charge as *"stored recreatable potentials of energy"* [2]. So it's a potential of energy and it's stored. We saw this in the example of the GPM: a battery which lasts forever. But how is charge re-created? How come it can be felt as a mass when it is only two postulates floating about which by themselves contain no mass at all?

How restimulation works and how masses are made after they were non-existent for ages, is explained in the "Factors", a set of theorems written by Hubbard as a *"summation of the consider-ations and examinations of the human spirit and the material uni-verse completed between A.D. 1923 and 1953"* [1]. (Theorems – as opposed to axioms – can be proven to be true, or disproven.)

The Factors describe an activity – any activity – from its begin-ning to its end in the sequence of **Be-Do-Have**. One has to **be** someone (a baker), then **do** what's appropriate (baking) and **have** a product (bread) as a result. This simple sequence is dif-ferentiated into thirty steps, Fac.1 to Fac.30.

When discussed on a high level of abstraction the Factors may provide answers concerning the creation of the physical uni-verse. In a way, they form a "quantum theory of the theta uni-verse" (comparable to the quantum theory of physics.) On a more practical level they would describe the steps inherent in running a business or – for our purposes – the coming and go-ing of mental mest.

To fully comprehend the mechanism of restimulation we must understand what attention is. Attention, according to the Fac-tors, consists of theta energy quanta or **attention units**. They are a somethingness, not a nothingness. They are, in whatever subtle way, "solid" (Fac. 13).

As one puts one's attention on things or people (whether they are in physical reach or not) one gets a sensation of either emo-tional closeness or distance with them. The higher one's affin-ity, i.e. the higher one's position on the tonescale regarding them, the closer one feels to them. Evidently, by putting one's attention on things, mental space is created. The dimensions of this space depend on the number of attention units one has put out and on their affinity value (e.g. interest, boredom, anger). Because they produce dimensions, attention units are referred to as **dimension points** in the Factors (Fac. 4).

Think of someone you like. What happens? You have him or her "in your space". You agree with her, she is real; there is the intention to give and receive communication. Regarding this person, you have a large space. Now think of someone you don't like. He is not so much in your space. You have put your dimension points "this side of him". You want to keep him out.

There is a certain degree of unreality i.e. disagreement connected with that person, and an unwillingness to communicate. – This was to demonstrate that mental **space** is created by dimension points, and that attention is not a neutral thing but a mental **energy** directly reflecting a position on the tone scale (Fac. 5-8).

Now lean back, close your eyes and think of a cat or a dog. Think of it in as many details as you can. Keep reaching, keep pouring out those attention units. The more you do this, the more "solid" the picture becomes. With this picture you have created mental **matter**. – Now withdraw your attention and thereby uncreate the picture. Ok. Reach for the picture again, re-create it. Look at a nice experience you had with this cat or dog. Look at some action. When you have done so, withdraw from the picture. – You have probably noticed that you could fit a two-hour walk with plenty of details into the five seconds you have spent looking at the picture. This is mental **time** (Fac. 14, 18).

Putting dimension points on things, places, people or animals means as much as establishing a **communication line** to them, be it in your mind or for real. Dimension points can be very solid, by the way. They may have the form of letters, spoken words, bullets, flowers, bank cheques, etc. All these things are means to give attention. They are the physical equivalent to your mental attention units and very much reveal your degree of affinity with the person. You never think of someone – you never send him a letter. It goes hand in hand.

What's on the other side of a communication line is called a **terminal**. Terminals are solid. They are people, animals, things or places. When you make them up in your mind by creating their picture they are terminals, too, because pictures are solid.

Now consider the terminals you can rely on and feel happy with. This gives you a sensation of stability. You feel well anchored in your space. This analogy of feeling anchored has lead to yet another name for our theta quanta, that of **anchor points**. Now think of someone who has given you a hard time recently. He has unstabilized your space by knocking your anchor points inwards. Your space lost dimension; when the going was rough it may have even collapsed. Accordingly, you would have felt quite misemotional.

Whether you say dimension point, attention unit or anchor point – they are all theta quanta. Hubbard used different words in the thirty years of his research to explain the same thing from different angles. And what are theta quanta? Simply what you need in order to communicate, at least in this universe. A thetan cannot "just so" talk to another thetan; he needs a relay point. A thetan without a relay point is no terminal. He is simply not there as a communication partner, in the same way as a company doesn't exist as long as it doesn't have a telephone, a mailing address and a letterbox (Fac. 11 and 24). In order to be there, he must first create a space and then take up a position in that space. Only then he can do something, e.g. communicate. The sequence always is: be – do – have. When a baker never created a bakery or happens not to be in it (be), he cannot bake (do) and there won't be any bread (have).

Now from where is this space created? Who or what feels well or not so well anchored? You, the thetan? Maybe, maybe not. It depends. We must differentiate here between you, the thetan who is cause over all this (Fac. 1), the beingness you have assumed in the game you were going to play (Fac. 2), and the viewpoint you are taking in this game (Fac. 3). To be strictly technical about it: space is created from your viewpoint. Dimension points are extended from the viewpoint, not from the beingness, not from the thetan (Fac. 4).

This was quite a mouthful. Let us find an example. There is a professor of physics, Mr. Quark. That's his beingness. He, the thetan, is beyond and above all roles and identifications. However, on the level of beingness or identity, he is a physics professor. He has some other beingnesses or identities, too: husband, father, golf player, and so on. One thetan, many beingnesses. With regard to each beingness, Mr. Quark holds certain viewpoints. There is more than one viewpoint to each being-ness. As a physics professor he holds several scientific view-points, debates them, defends them, uses them to knock the anchorpoints of his opponents in by skillful argumentation, changes them when they have become untenable. He is well known for his ability to hold his position against scientific attacks and criticisms. His space is very stable there. His view-point is well anchored. He is not so good holding his position against his teenage daughter. She somehow manages to make him change his viewpoint in her favour, no matter how much he tries to be fierce and say "no". His space (his "fatherly authority") easily gets a dent with her. There are frequent shouting matches. But as he generally adores her, there is no harm done and he quickly recovers. Things are different in golf-ing. His space collapses like a ton of bricks coming down when he plays a ball badly and loses a round. He goes off fu-ming, doesn't recover for hours, and is considered unbearable by everybody around. He takes golf seriously and puts a lot of effort into it. When he has won he walks around with his chest blown up like a balloon and is considered equally unbearable by everybody around.

To sum it up: one's space widens and shrinks as one reaches and withdraws. The dimensions of one's space (its size) corre-spond to the tonescale, i.e. the affinity level one has concern-ing the terminal in question. As long as one remains pan-deter-mined, one can be responsible for both sides of a game simul-taneously. One stays aloof and plays one's beingness plus corre-sponding viewpoints "from above", like a puppet player. (Mr. Quark well manages to do so as a scientist. He can accept it to drop or change viewpoints without getting a personal feeling of loss. Tonelevel: interest). When one's space gets shaken one tends to become self-determined and identify with one's being-ness. (To his daughter, Mr. Quark is very much a father who is trying to keep his self-determinism. He does mind losing his viewpoint on her, even though he may recover easily. Regar-ding her, he is not above things. Tonelevel: antagonism.) When one's space gets shaken really badly, one may go as far as identifying with the viewpoint in order to defend it. (When Mr. Quark plays golf he is so nervous that he is soldered right up inside his skull and the space he has is limited to the distance between his eyes and the golfball, and his whole attention is lasered into this single terminal, the golf ball. This is fixated attention and self-determinism at its worst. Tonelevel: fear.) On the levels of other-determinism and below one wouldn't even have a viewpoint of one's own anymore. One would accept the viewpoint indoctrinated upon one by another. No self-created dimensions, no own space. And, of course, irresponsibility.

MENTAL UNIVERSES

Up to this point we have been talking only about the world of Mr. Quark without considering anyone else. All the spaces created from the different viewpoints of Mr. Quark's various beingnesses add up to his **universe**. The dictionary defines "universe" as "the whole of existing things". Hubbard defines it as *"a whole system of created things"* [2]. This is in keeping with the framework of his philosophy which states that before there was a somethingness (and be it only one single theta quantum) there was a nothingness (the thetan in his non-identified static state), and it is the nothingness which created the somethingness. In simpler terms: before there was mest, there was theta; before there was a physical universe, there was the spirit. All things start with a thought, a postulate, an intention.

Mr. Quark would speak of his universe as the "first universe". Yet he is not alone in the world. Other people have beingnesses and viewpoints and dimension points and spaces, and the dimension points interact because people give each other attention, build up and knock down each other's spaces, viewpoints and beingnesses – in a word, from this interaction we get all the phenomena there are to communication, and they occur between **three universes**. *"The universes, then, are three in number: the universe created by one viewpoint, the universe created by every other viewpoint, the universe created by the mutual action of* *viewpoints which is agreed to be upheld (. . .)"* (Fac. 23). Example: Mr. Quark develops a new concept in physics (first universe). It refers to the already existing body of data which has been accumulated for centuries by the mutual efforts of physicists. Some of these data are thoroughly agreed upon, others are being looked at skeptically (third universe). Mr. Quark communicates his new concept to a colleague, i.e. he intends to create a duplication and understanding of what he thinks (first universe) in the mind of the other (second universe). His colleague gets the point (duplication, understanding), and can agree to some of it. Now the two of them have something in common. To that extent a third universe has been formed. – Quite obviously the phenomena connected with ARC and the communication formula apply to all three universes.

This game of coming to an agreement by throwing together dimension points has one disadvantage: they are hard to take apart because in the end one can't tell any more which dimension point has which owner – particularly when some owners deny they are the owners, or when some others (power-greedy ones) put a false claim of ownership there. This leads to all the problems connected with responsibility and playing games. Example: Mrs. Quark has an outdoors picnic to celebrate Mr. Quark's scientific breakthrough. When it's finished the grass is littered with paper, plastic cups, bottles, etc. Quite visibly, an agreed-upon space has been created by these dimension points. Mrs. Quark stands up and says: "All right everybody, let's all take care of our rubbish. Each of you pick up what you have dropped on the grass and take it to the nearest rubbish bin on the way back." Five minutes of activity ensue. The amount of litter has not decreased markedly. How come? Well, some of the people had left already and for their bits nobody felt any responsibility, other people forgot what they threw down, others again said they hadn't when in fact they had. This of course makes the rubbish persist (Ax. 29).

Another trap brought about by grouping dimension points and creating things out of them is the phenomenon of scarcity. Take

118

an artist: He may consider his creation so valuable that he would regret to sell it. Which means that he has lost his belief in his ability to create in abundance, to create the same and even better things in the future. He has started invalidating his potential. This is the moment when he will introvert into the creation. He literally will lose his viewpoint and "become the thing". He will live not as himself but as "his creation". He will be the caricature of what's known as a "real artist". This being-ness he did not assume in the deliberate way characteristic for high tonescale positions, but compulsively and in the spirit of defeat. And because the dimension points and therefore the whole creation may perish the thetan thinks he is likely to perish, too. Thus the idea of death comes about. (Fac. 18, 19, 24.)

RESTIMULATION

Having clarified the concept of mental mest and universes we may now leave Mr. Quark, his wife and her picnic and return to the problem of restimulation.

To start with an example: there is Mr. Bush, a wealthy London businessman. Although he has the money for it he never lives in a house of his own, he prefers apartments. Large, lush, luxurious apartments. He loves gold and marble. He feels a mixture of grief and elatedness when he is surrounded by gold and marble. His wife would like to live out in the country. She nags him to buy one of those quaint manor houses down in Sussex. It would be just the house of her dreams. He invariably gets short-tempered on the subject and tells her that it isn't worth bothering with as "one never gets what one wants anyway". At long last the tenacity of his wife does the trick. He buys her a manor house, stables, gatehouse, garden and all. The first summer they spend there he gets very depressed. He keeps grumbling about the building, its shape, location, cost of upkeep. Invariably he throws in the comment that you don't get what you want anyway. To overcome his depressions he seeks refuge in drinking too much. As well he develops a fascination for photo albums depicting classical Moghul architecture. "That's the sort of thing one ought to have," he says whilst helping himself to another drink, "but one never gets what one wants anyway". Mr. Bush is at the point of turning into an alcoholic. He is persuaded to get treatment and moves to his London flat for the time he sees his psychoanalyst. After two weeks – without any consultations – his symptoms disappear. His depressions subside and he goes back to his occasional social drinking.

As you have probably guessed: Mr. Bush and Gopdhal Khan are one and the same person. Between the two lifetimes there are a good 350 years. There were a number of other lifetimes as well, but they don't count regarding this subject of restimulation. The charge on palaces lay dormant for 350 years; now it has become activated. Result: depressions and a compulsion to drink alcohol.

How was this restimulation caused? By Mr. Bush putting attention on this postulate pair, this GPM. He for some reason was never before in the position to consider buying the house of his (or his wife's) dreams. There were maybe minor incidents in past lives where a bit of charge flared up, but nothing that would have seriously touched him. But in this case now, he couldn't help putting attention on his wife's wish to have the house of her dreams. Well, all right then, he thinks, if that's what she wants. They go, look around a bit, and buy one. This activity made Mr. Bush outflow attention units on his own first postulate ("dream house"), and this was immediately followed by the appearance of the second postulate ("you never get what you want"). But then again he *would* like to make his dream come true (attention on that), but oh no, it won't work ever (attention on that). Well it might work (attention on that). No, because one never gets what one wants (attention on that). There is a mechanism building up whereby Mr. Bush gets into a "flip-flop" between one postulate and the other. There is a compulsive "can't have" and a compulsive "must have" and he can't help extending his dimension points to these two GPM postulates simply because the source of restimulation is right there in his present environement – in the form of the actual manor house in which they both live. And as all dimension points are solid (as we saw), this accumulation of dimension points builds up to a mass, a mental mass. And in this mass is reflected the emotion of loss and grief of 1628, when he found his palace burnt down, and the subsequent apathy which he soothed with hasheesh then (and which leads to his alcoholism of today).

As soon as attention is put on a GPM, it all comes to life again: postulates, considerations, time, place, form and event, attitudes, emotions, sensations and pains. The whole incident. Reason: the original incident was centered around Gopdhal Khan's alter-is postulate and succumb to the circumstances. He refused to confront that his palace had burnt down. He could not have it be that way. By "hiding" behind a self-created wall of dimension points (or theta energy quanta) he tried to keep this unwanted reality away from himself. This way a "photographic film" was made upon which time, place, form and event of the incident were recorded. The more resistence, the more film, the more solid the picture. It is a theta energy film. It is held up by the two postulates left and right. If there weren't two postulates there would be no film. As soon as the GPM is restimulated, i.e. as soon as theta quanta are flowing towards it, the film reels off again. The pc "reads it off the screen" when he is in session. Out of session, when he is not concentrating fully, he may only get the emotions, sensations and psychosomatic pains of it, but none of its visual content. He may reactively voice the second postulate (as Mr. Bush did) but won't be aware of this (Dn Ax. 144).

Let us use a comparison here: imagine the two postulates to be two invisible flag poles. They are invisible because postulates have no mass, and cannot be seen in the form of pictures. Before the incident there is only one flagpole – the 1st postulate. At the moment of the incident, when the thetan gives up, the 2nd postulate is made. This gives us the second flagpole. In between there is a banner on which the entire incident with all its 55 perceptics is being "imprinted". The banner consists of theta energy quanta by which the thetan is trying to block off the unwanted experience. Once the incident is over the thetan calms down (destimulation); the banner is folded up and put away; what's left, are two invisible flagpoles. At the moment of restimulation – whoosh! – the banner unfolds all by itself; the incident has come back into the present. Sometimes it is even more real than the present, depending on how long and how intensely the thetan was exposed to the banner. – So, and now we know what Hubbard means when he says that charge is "stored re-creatable potentials of energy".

Supposing you were auditing Mr. Bush on this, when would the session be over? As soon as Mr. Bush had recognized his alter-is postulate and taken full responsibility for it: "Yes, that's it; that's what I thought then. Isn't that just amazing! Wasn't that a great way of falling over my own feet!" (Laughs). This will make the second postulate vanish. Now he can act upon the 1st postulate and accept the house he has bought as a dream house or go off and build or buy the real thing. As well Mr. Bush could acknowledge the fact that this postulate of "I want to have the house of my dreams" indeed exists; he could admire it for what it is, admire himself for having made such a postulate – and make it vanish, too. That would complete the whole cycle; he would no longer have any attention on "dream houses". (Fac. 14, 29.)

Auditing is the process of getting the pc to build up ARC with the GPMs in his mind. As soon as he has found the second postulate he is able to causatively look at the pictures connected with it and may re-create them at will any time (as an act of memory). At this moment the compulsive re-creation imposed on him by the existence of the second postulate, becomes impossible. There can only be one thing at a time: either the compulsive creation or his causative self-creation. And once he can do it causatively the compulsion goes forever. (Ax. 12, 20.)

"Ax. 24: Total ARC would bring about the vanishment of all mechanical conditions of existence." (Mental masses, misemotions as well as alcoholism are "mechanical conditions of existence".)

"Ax. 30: The general rule of auditing is that anything which is unwanted and yet persists must be thoroughly viewed, at which time it will vanish." Evidently, the way out of the whole problem is having a great ability to confront and enough ARC to become bigger than one's GPMs.

HAVINGNESS

There is still one unanswered question: how can one keep oneself from getting into trouble in the first place? – Answer: by being able to have nothing, by being able to be comfortable with nothing.

This is very hard to confront. Gopdhal Khan wanted to have a something (the dream palace), wasn't able to tolerate a nothing (when he found his place burnt down), and out of that arose a compulsive reach and withdraw, a "must have/can't have" GPM.

At first glance Havingness means no more than *"ARC with the environment"* [2]. The more real something is to you, the more you like it, the easier you can have it around or do something with it. Whatever you have a lot of ARC with, you can "have" a lot. You feel comfortable with it, you can reach it easily, and feel supported by it. You feel "good" about it, and we could say your "Havingness is high" on it.

So Havingness is a constantly changing state and measures the degree of ARC one has. When you cannot "have" something, and resist it, you build up charge. On the other hand, if you can stomach it easily when something unwanted occurs or when you lose something, no charge is built up. Havingness therefore can be the result of the communication with something *or* of the communication with nothing. Therefore, in essence, it is a measure of one's *ability* to communicate with something or nothing. If this communication ability is inhibited, charge is generated.

This concept of Havingness is one of the pivots of Hubbard's philosophy. One rather conclusive statement is to be found in "Ability Magazine 34", 1956 [20]. There he describes Havingness as a paradox: you have an infinite being, the thetan, who for some reason has put it into his mind that he should communicate (1st postulate). That's fine. No paradox yet. He is all right as long as he doesn't mind communicating without anyone listening, i.e. without a terminal. He has endless space and his communication pervades it, goes all the way through it, from one end of infinity to the other. He has a great time. Until he decides that he must communicate *to* a terminal! (2nd postulate, alter-is). Now he has set himself up for a loss. He doesn't simply want to communicate any more for the sake of communication, he wants to create an effect. And worse, he wants admiration for it, applause, cheers. This way, he makes himself dependent on a terminal.

Terminals, per definition, are always solid. They are the communication relay points between two thetans. A "pure" thetan is, by definition, no terminal as he has no vibration, no mass, no energy, no location in space (Ax. 44). He must produce these to be locatable. For two thetans to communicate with each other there must be a relay system; this job is done by the dimension points. The two thetans communicate *via* something. When you make a mistake in this arrangement, the relay system will become more important than the person you are talking to: this way souvenirs and relics come about. They are symbols of past communications; they are enshrined relay points. You venerate *them* instead of who used to be "on the other side" of them (Fac. 11, 24; Ax. 25).

What is between you and me? Paper and black ink. In order that I may communicate my thoughts to you, we need to have this relay system. Should I wish to talk to you, we would have to bring our bodies into an appropriate position, use vocal chords, produce sound waves, set ear drums in motion, activate neural synapses, etc. All these aids come under the heading of "dimension points". Anything we use as a means of communication becomes a dimension point – be it bodies, tanks, enemy armies, letters, flowers, crystal balls or horoscopes.

And here, finally, we have the paradox: there is a nothingness (the thetan) who requires being acknowledged by a somethingness (the terminal) to confirm that he (the thetan) exists.

Whoever has a problem with regard to having Nothing, needs Something: a terminal. If there isn't one, he will create one: by putting out a dimension point, and another one and another one, and he'll make them nice and solid and now he has someone to talk to. This is how he creates his first universe. (When you see people talking to themselves they are just busy communicating to a made-up terminal.)

The whole problem is summed up in this statement: *"The highest purpose in this universe is the creation of an effect"* (Ax. 10). It is so much easier to have something instead of nothing, to communicate to a somethingness instead of a nothingness, that the thetan permits himself to get pulled down into the realm of matter, energy, space and time (mental as well as physical) in order to have fun. Which is safe as long as he does not introvert into the mest universe and get stuck there. As long as he can have the loss of terminals and dimension points (e.g. friends or money), i.e. can have nothing where before there was something, he won't get trapped by his own compulsive flip-flop of "must have/ can't have". As long as he does not forget that there is a whole abundance of terminals and dimension points he could create for himself (make new friends, make more money, etc), he will never have a loss. It is all a matter of certainty of self (Fac. 28).

So what's the answer to "avoidance of charge"? Simply this: Know that having nothing is not a threat to you because you can always create some more of something. So there is no loss, no failed purpose, no frustration, no dimishing and degrading of self by making counter-postulates to your original postulates, no charge generated. Know that you are infinite and immortal and that survival problems therefore are paradoxical. Know that playing a game happens within the framework of matter, energy, space and time, but know as well that you as a thetan exist outside matter, energy, space and time. – When you can hold this attitude you have attained "serenity of being", at tone 40 of the emotional tone scale.

The Key Terms of Auditing

ENGRAMS, IMPLANTS AND GPMS

In dianetics there are three categories of incidents, graded according to their heaviness: engrams, secondaries and locks. Their definitions follow in the course of this text. An **engram** is the heaviest. It is a *"mental image picture which is a recording of a time of physical pain and unconsciousness"* [2]. It contains as well a recording of a second postulate. This is why it contains charge at all. The body suffered it; the thetan made the postulate. Falling off roofs, breaking one's legs, operations, illnesses, accidents are all incidents which may be recorded as engrams. Please note that the incidents themselves are not engrams. The *recordings* of them are, though. They are done the moment a thetan agrees that there is a stop to his intentions and actions. If he could easily tolerate the accident or injury or implant, die, go exterior, and say "I'll carry on anyway", it wouldn't be an engram. So the necessary ingredient for an incident to be recorded as an engram isn't just pain and unconsciousness, but the succumb postulate made before or during the incident.

Hubbard calls engrams *"the single source of all inorganic mental and organic psycho-somatic ills"* [3]. They work this way after the principle: you become what you resist. The very parts of the engram incident which you cannot confront, are recorded by the ridge you have formed in your defense. And precisely what you don't want you'll get – because you'll carry it with you in form of the picture you made. When your car swerved and turned over, you thought: "I don't want to die!" Each time this gets restimulated, you'll feel fear of death. You think: "What a terrible awful splintered bone! I can't get myself to look at it!" – Of all the broken bones, that's the one which will *not* set right. You pretend things weren't the way they are, you alter-is them and – wham! – there's a ridge recording the whole thing and playing it back on you mentally or physically. (For plenty more examples, see DMSMH [3].)

As the GPM and the two postulates contained therein are the backbone of our further discussions regarding the practice of auditing, there is a quick "rule of thumb" definition to remind you: 1st postulate: reach, start, above antagonism on the tone-scale (as-isness). 2nd postulate: withdraw, stop, succumb, antagonism or below (alter-isness). GPM (Goals Problems Mass): the mass resulting from the tension between the two.

All engrams contain succumb postulates. Yet succumb postulates may as well occur without any *physical* pain and unconsciousness. After all, before there were bodies thetans already existed, played games and had their problems with them. This is what the term "GPM" refers to. It applies to the thetan as such. The term "engram" applies not only to the thetan-plus-body compound, but as well to the body *without* thetan, since it may have been recorded on the level of the **Genetic Entity (GE)** mentioned in Part One. No matter if you, the thetan, consider it a stop or not when your body gets smashed up – the body itself, the organism, does mind. *"The word engram in dianetics is used in its severely accurate sense as a "definite and permanent trace left by a stimulus on the protoplasm of a tissue". It is considered as a unit group of stimuli impinged solely on the cellular being"* (DMSMH, p.60).

In auditing it may therefore happen that the GE shoves an incident into the awareness of the thetan, i.e. an incident which was recorded by the GE and not by the thetan himself. It won't be difficult for the pc to tell them apart, as he feels "stand-off-ish" with the GE one; regarding his own he accepts the ownership. It is *his* incident, not a foreign-made one. And he knows it.

An **Implant** is a special form of engram or GPM, respectively. The difference lies in the underlying incident. Let's take a normal engram to start with. Situation one: you had an accident, the body lies next to the car and is unconscious, you as a thetan are pretty groggy, too. You think the body may die and postulate: "Oh it's over, I can feel it – I'm going to die!" – This is your 2nd postulate against the 1st postulate of thinking you'll live forever no matter how racily you may drive. Situation two: the ambulance comes, they get out to pick you up, one of them says: "Pretty bad". You, being rather confused, take that as a stable datum for yourself to hold on to, and think "pretty bad" as your second postulate. Before you thought you were pretty good, now you think you are pretty bad. The point here is that you picked up the postulate of another, agreed with it and made it your own.

In an engram, therefore, a second postulate is either made by you yourself or accidentally picked up from another. In an implant, the postulate is intentionally given to you by another. That's the whole purpose of an implant. *"A painful and forceful means of overwhelming a being with artificial purpose or false concepts in a malicious attempt to control and suppress him"* [2]. A really effective implant gives you postulates as well as counter-postulates regarding a preferably wide area of game. This way there is a good chance that it will be restimulated without your being able to escape that restimulation. The wider the area of game being addressed, the better the implant works. You can't withdraw – except inwards. So you introvert and become very small and stop playing games. Which is what was wanted.

A classical implant runs more or less like this: you sit strapped to your chair, electronic gear and picture flashing apparatus all around you, electrodes fastened to your temples. You get your shock, lose all orientation, become totally overwhelmed, and right then there is this voice into your ear: "be nobody" – shock – "be everybody" – shock – "do right" – shock – "do wrong" – shock, and so on. After that pretty much everything you try to be or do will be restimulative of the pains received and give you a headache. Your own viewpoint has been submerged by forcefully installed other viewpoints. You have become other-determined or even robotized. Drugs and hypnosis may be used as part of it.

You may wonder, but engrams/GPMs like this do come up in auditing. Apart from "whole track" incidents, versions of this range from supposedly "corrective" psychiatric treatment to brainwashing. The fact that early dianetics exposed such treatments in the attempt to resolve the problem of US war veterans may have played a part in the initial opposition to dianetics and scientology.

There is as well a lighter and more every-day version, called "teaching by engrams". Here is how it goes: little kid walks through a puddle, messes up her new shoes. Mother slaps her. "You don't want to walk in puddles (slap), do you!! (Slap) And you won't mess up your shoes again (slap), promise? (Slap)." – Makes good and solid citizens, this.

UNCONSCIOUSNESS

A note on the "unconsciousness" which forms part of the definition of engram: who goes unconscious – the body or the thetan? If it were the body and the thetan stayed fully conscious, he would then be able to recall it all. So there wouldn't be any engram on him, but maybe on the GE. If it were the thetan going unconscious. but how does a thetan go unconscious? – This is a matter of definition. Hubbard looks at unconsciousness as a gradual phenomenon. It is a sliding scale between full awareness and no awareness. Full awareness means 100% confront (free theta, free attention units) and duplication of what's going on; no awareness means no confront, no duplication.

A useful term to describe the phenomenon of unconsciousness is **randomity**. Randomity means, in the dictionary sense of the word: things are not happening by plan but by chance. Hubbard defines it from the subjective viewpoint of a person as *"theamount of predicted and unpredicted motion"* a person can tolerate [2]. It's a proportion between the two. When one can predict most of what's going on one feels bored. This would be **minus randomity** (Dn Ax. 73). When it's a nice mixture between predictability and surprise, one feels interested and entertained. This would be called **optimum randomity**. When too much goes on – more than one could grasp – one feels overwhelmed and loses control. This is called **plus randomity**. Naturally, it all depends on the confronting ability someone has. What a racing driver would consider minus randomity probably is totally overwhelming (plus randomity) to most people.

Back to unconsciousness: *"Dn Ax.93: Unconsciousness is an excess of randomity imposed by a counter-effort of sufficient force to cloud the awareness (.)."* When the thetan loses track of what is happening but canot withdraw, he goes to that degree unconscious of his environment and his body. He loses his viewpoint partly or wholly; he withdraws dimension points and his space shrinks. This may occur when there is too much happening, but as well when there is too little happening. *"Dn Ax 92: The engram is a severe area of plus or minus randomity of sufficient volume to cause unconsciousness."*

It is easy to imagine how plus randomity would cause one to lose control and cloud one's awareness. One was busy fighting things, and there was just too much happening all at the same time. A car crash would be a good example. You just can't follow *all* of the motions suddenly reeling off all around you with lightning speed.

A situation of severe *minus* randomity which may cloud one's awareness is probably less obvious. Therefore an example: the jet-fighter pilot who was shot out of his damaged plane, came down on a parachute and now sits in the middle of the Sahara desert with absolutely nothing happening – that's the start of a GPM and an engram! Leaving his plane and parachuting down had high randomity, but he could handle that easily. No shock, no engram conected with this. But with the desert, with sitting and waiting, yes, there is an engram conected with this. Why? Because he has all the time in the world to very slowly succumb to the circumstances and make a good and strong counter-postulate against flying in general and deserts in particular. There is absolutely nothing else to attract his attention except his own mishap and his fruitless efforts to make it un-happen. He introverts and goes unconscious of his environment. What is hard on him as a thetan, is the minus-randomity. Because of it, he forms a GPM. Parallel to that his body dies of of thirst and sunburn. On a cellular level there is a lack of supplies, so the GE suffers from minus-randomity as well. It records a physical engram in the sense of "memory traces left on the cells".

How are things recorded when he goes unconscious? Well, he may not take it all in as it is happening. In the case of the car crash, death comes too fast; in the case of the pilot, death comes too slow. In any case: the thetan is always there pouring out attention, intention, theta energy and dimension points to keep the worst from happening, or to call up the powers which may save him. He is pushing out and pulling in, thereby producing the film the whole thing is being recorded on. The less he confronts, the more he resists and the more film is put there. The more he confronts, the less he resists and the less film is put there. In this latter case the person will have no pictures of the incident. He knows it happened, oh yes, and he can talk about it with no charge. And with no pictures. The other person involved in the car crash referred to above, couldn't confront looking at it when it happened, and can't do so now either. She just can't get herself to talk about it. She's surrounded by pictures, ridges, masses and energies, all too terrible to look at. Full-blown restimulation. Takes 15 hours of auditing to run her through the whole thing, make her confront it layer by layer, until finally she finds the counterpostulate she made in the incident. The incident discharges; now she laughs about it. She knows it happened and can talk about it in detail with no charge. Like the other person. Except he needed no auditing; she did. Difference in confront level and availability of free theta, that's the reason. (Please note that this is only true for the thetan himself. The GE *always* records, because it *always* resists, whatever may be countering physical survival. This is a "built-in construction feature". The GE is made that way.)

SECONDARIES AND LOCKS

Having cleared "engram" and "unconsciousness" we are now going to look at the remaining two categories of incidents.

They are called "secondary" for the lighter category and "lock" for the lightest category.

A **secondary** is the restimulation of the loss contained in the engram. *"The secondary engram depends for its strength and force upon physical pain engrams which underlie it."* [2]

After all, by making a 2nd postulate the thetan has given up his own self-determined goal; he has lost his game and therefore lost what he considered a survival thing to do. He may have lost his body, too. His survival potential has decreased. An incident restimulating his loss of a body or a game will cause grief, sadness, tears. These are the typical phenomena for a secondary.

A **lock** is as well the restimulation of a loss or stop, but of a lighter kind than the secondary. The phenomena are: slight misemotion, an uncomfortable wondering about something one was impressed with. A "button" has been pushed, the thetan doesn't quite know why he went downtone all of a sudden, and he wonders about it. Locks are moments when dormant engrams are woken up for a short moment and conect up with the thetan.

VALENCES

Picking up a postulate from another is called "going into his valence". Derived from the Latin word for "power", the term "valence" means as much as becoming part of another's power and therefore losing one's own . When you, with a lot of affinity, assume the viewpoint of another, that's taking on a beingness. That is *not* a valence shift. However, when you, in a state of unconsciousness and overwhelm, become indoctrinated with the postulates of another, that *is* going into the other's valence. Identifying with a **winning valence** really is a survival choice done on an aberrated level: "If he is so strong that he can kill me, he must be a better survivor than I am, therefore it's safer to become him than to stay myself".

133

Example: It is the year 1327, a portly monk is being robbed and killed by two robbers. One of the two, just as he brings down the deathly blow, shouts: "I'll show you, priest!" This robber is a skinny man who wears a huge beard and a red scarf. In this incident there are three valences, three "dramatis personae": the monk, the bearded one and the second robber. The second robber is the weakest valence, simply because he keeps himself in the background. The fight happens between the monk and the bearded robber. Here the monk is the loser. As he dies, he thinks: "Its all over now!" The strongest valence is the bearded robber. He is the winner. Sixhundred and fifty years later, in 1977, we meet the monk again. His name is Frank Rogers now; he belongs to a left-wing intellectual group who specialises in denouncing religion as opium for the people. Frank Rogers is rather portly; he wears a red scarf and a huge beard. He is known for his wild anti-clerical utterances; his favourite is: "Just you wait, you priests, we'll show you!" Comrades close to him, however, can't help but recognize a tendency towards despair beneath his wildness; any slightest mishap will make him believe that "it's all over now". Obviously, two valences are being dramatized here: the winning one (the robber) and Frank's own (the monk). Both are overlapping; that of the robber is in the foreground. Being rough and tough, believes Frank, is the best way to make it in life.

Our example demonstrates how valences can show themselves in mannerisms and in voicing one's 2nd postulates without noticing. These go around one's heads in ever repeating **circuits** and cause the phenomenon of inner voices, sometimes so strongly that it seems like a little **demon** was talking. Indeed, occasionally one may feel a voice coming down from the left or from some ten feet above, for example. In any case you are dealing with **entities** which are nothing but ridges. They contain pictures and postulates acting as "voices".
Of course one may consciously put on a valence, like in acting. This contains the potential liability of restimulating the exist-

ing valences in the case. One may have a hard time stripping off the role one played once one is off the stage!

ANALYTICAL MIND – REACTIVE MIND

The model of "analytical mind" and "reactive mind", presented in 1950 in the book "Dianetics", has lead to a lot of confusion because it was taken literally and resulted in the idea that the thetan thinks "with" his analytical mind and is restimulated because he has engrams "in" his reactive mind. Auditing – on this level of literalness – is understood as a process whereby one takes the black nasty pictures "out of" the reactive mind, cleans them off by looking at them carefully and then puts the nice pretty pictures "in" the analytical mind.

This is great for a simple and descriptive model, but that's not the way it works. An engram is restimulated by stimuli in the thetan's environment, yes, he finds himself doing and saying things he couldn't agree with once the restimulation is over, yes, but the engrams are not "in" his reactive mind. The reactive mind consists of all the GPMs and ridges and circuits and valences and entities (which is all the same anyway); it consists of them but it does not *contain* these things. What makes the thetan react is one or more GPMs in sudden or chronic restimulation. A GPM consists of two postulates. Postulates don't exist inside anything, that's totally against their definition. The pictures and masses re-created at the moment of restimulation which make the thetan react, are not inside anything either; much rather they are around the body – which is where the thetan has his viewpoint usually – and press in on it. When the thetan leaves his body he takes his mind along. His mind consists of *"pictures (. . .) preserved in energy and mass in the vicinity of the being (. . .) which when restimulated are re-created without his analytical awareness"* [2].

The analytical mind consists of the circuits the thetan has made up voluntarily in order to put certain activities "on automatic", such as writing, driving a car, swimming, etc. They are the result of learning. The thetan does not think "with" his analytical mind. *He* thinks. And the analytical mind he *uses*. He uses it as a *"communication and control system between the thetan and his environment"* [2].

Without a mind the thetan could not be contacted; he simply wouldn't be there. In order to be in the game, he needs a mind; without his mind he would be static. The mind is actually nothing else but the viewpoint the thetan takes within a universe. The difference between thetan and mind is not always made in common scientologese parlance – not even by Hubbard himself. On the one hand he says: *"In the final analysis, what is this thing called thetan? It is you before you mocked yourself up"* [2]. Thereby the thetan is positioned above the "mocked-up self". This "self" corresponds to the analytical mind: *"The awareness of awareness unit plus some evaluative circuits or machinery to make the handling of the body possible"* [2]. Therefore the analytical mind is not the thetan (the awareness of awareness unit) in his pure form, but the thetan *plus* something. Yet on the other hand, and quite in violation of this, Hubbard says: *"The analytical mind is just the pc, the thetan"* [2].

In this text, we will stick to this last definition because it has come to be generally used amongst scientologists. When we say "thetan", we mean the active player (Fac. 2); when we say "the static", we refer to him who is "before the beginning" (Fac. 1).

Another hint with regard to the differentiation beween static, mind and reactive mind is given by the definition of **bank**. The term is taken in analogy to the data-banks of computers. It means *"a combination of energy and significance and this comprises a mass (. . .)"* [2]. What then does the bank, or the reactive mind, consist of? Of aberrated postulates (significances) and masses (pictures). And the analytical mind? Of sensible postulates and pictures. And the static? Of none of all that.

KEY-IN AND KEY-OUT

As we have already seen in Part One, the bank is the total sum of GPMs; the **case**, however, is the sum of only those which are in restimulation. This means that case exists at any given moment only to the extent that the reactive bank is restimulated. People are more or less "casey" depending on how many restimulators are present and how worn out they are. Being worn out they have little free theta left and react to pretty much anything. This is why a change of environment or a holiday may work wonders – until one is back in the old environment and the old restimulators start working on one again.

GPMs not currently restimulated lie "dormant". Therefore a person who lives in a safe and stable environment may appear very bright and happy and case-less. Here a change of environment may work very much to his detriment. He may **key in** all sorts of engrams and GPM postulate pairs. "Key in" (again a computer term) means: the moment the GPM is restimulated and the flip-flop set off. When this particular person comes back home (lives in the country, has been in the city for two weeks visiting relatives; comes back as a nervous wreck), she will slowly **key out**. This means that the various GPMs which were keyed in in the city slowly or gradually stop flip-flopping. When it's over, that's the moment of key-out.

An **erasure** is achieved when the GPM- or engram-forming incident has been found, fully confronted and duplicated, and when the 2nd postulate made then has been as-ised. A key-out, in contrast, is the dropping away of the GPM because enough theta has been regained by whatever means to "cut the wire". (Child cries, gets an icecream, stops crying. A key-out.) An erasure means: going all the way to the source of the trouble.

A GPM therefore is the **basic on the chain**. Whenever it is restimulated, an enturbulation of theta occurs and is recorded as a secondary or lock. The incidents related to one particular GPM make a **chain**. It is a chain only of those incidents which are connected to this particular GPM. The aim in auditing is to find and discharge incidents working back along a single chain to the basic, which will erase. One danger one may run into in auditing, is the "crossing of chains", caused by the pc starting to freely associate rather than looking for the exact earlier similar incident. The pc then gets so massy as if someone had poured concrete all over him, and the session gets stuck.

When the free theta of the pc is low, he may have to run through each incident on the chain from the present to the past in order to get down to the basic. When he has a lot of free theta, he will blow through the whole chain at first glance, find the basic and come up with the postulate right away (Dn Ax. 124).

END PHENOMENA

A moment like the one just mentioned would be considered an **end phenomenon (EP)**. It is characterized by a **cognition**, which is a realization about his life after the aberrating postulate has been as-ised, and **VGIs** (Very Good Indicators, i.e. pc looks bright). On the E-meter you would see a certain needle phenomenon called "floating needle" (see Part Three). Not only an erasure, but a key-out, too, is an end phenomenon. Naturally, it is not as thorough as an erasure. Many key-outs, however, make the person regain so much free theta that he floats off like a balloon and totally disconnects from the bank. This is called a **release**.

Some pc's cannot have it that a cycle of action is complete. They cannot have that there all of a sudden is nothing where before there was something (the GPM). So they keep on looking – and restimulate some other GPM by means of the power of their attention. This is called an **overrun**. The pc "pulls in masses" again – from somewhere else. The auditor has to be very careful not to allow the pc to overrun. Although one can easily rehabilitate the EP which occurred before the moment of overrun, it means that the auditor lacks session control.

138

THE COMPOSITE CASE

In Part One the fact was mentioned that ridges may be made by one person but picked up by another later on. This means that *not* all GPMs, ridges, engrams, valences and circuits one carries around as part of one's case ,were fabricated by oneself. One may have – at some time or other – contacted some foreign-made ones and "woken them up" by one's attention. The ensuing restimulation one of course did not like but resisted it and tried to push the source of it out of one's space. Which of course made it connect up even stronger.

So there is one's "own case" (consisting of home-made ridges) and there is the **composite case** (consisting of foreign-made ones one went in contact with). The ridges in the composite case are usually referred to as **entities**. Some people can "see" entities naturally, others learn to do so as they move up the auditing steps to Clear and above.

The Rudiments of Life

THE "RUDIMENTS"

In the friction between an as-isness and an alter-isness, in the lie implied by an alter-isness, we have the most fundamental violation of one's personal integrity. There is something one has considered true and now one doesn't consider it true any more – just because there is a barrier consisting of matter, energy, space or time. One has allowed the mest universe to be bigger than oneself; one has invalidated one's position (as a thetan) outside and above mest and one has done so knowingly. That's pretty bad. Putting one's own certainty (1st universe) in question and succumbing to the mest universe (3rd universe) – that is the fundamental overt act a thetan could commit. The term **overt**, in scientologese, stands for any kind of misdeed. It is called an overt because you cannot deny to yourself that you did it – even when there was no witness about.

Certainty in the first universe may not mean that something is certain to happen in the third universe, i.e. "objectively". One may be certain that one's car won't get stolen (first universe) although everyone around tells one that it's silly to leave it out in the street and one should put it in a garage. Eventually it does get stolen (third universe). Now they'll all say: "Didn't we know it! See how wrong you were to act against our advice". One doesn't have to feel wrong at all, actually. One stuck to one's certainty, that's all. One didn't allow "public opinion" to destabilize one in one's certainty. Now that the car has been stolen – ok, one takes the hint and puts the next car in a garage. But one changed one's opinion *oneself*, that's the point. First one was certain it wasn't going to get stolen, now one is certain that cars do get stolen in this part of town. One has lived by one's own truth and experience. Had one listened to the others and put the car away one might have felt a little stupid, like: "Why do I rent this expensive garage when I don't even know if cars get stolen around here? How do I know if these people are right or wrong?"

One had to test it out and match one's own certainty against the 3rd universe. One made one's experiences and adjusted one's postulates accordingly. But not in the spirit of defeat! Not as a 2nd postulate! One found a new survival course after finding the previous survival course unworkable. So one "officially" ended the original consideration and replaced it by a new consideration. There is a difference between "wishful thinking" which lives off drawing the curtains on the harshness of reality, and sensibly postulating *in accordance* with reality. A matter of good confront, as usual. *"Logic 16: An abstract postulate must be compared to the universe to which it applies and brought into the category of things which can be sensed, measured or experienced in that universe before such postulate can be considered workable."* [1]

The art of "living by as-isness" would imply that one always ends a cycle of action. One would either fulfill or un-create a postulate, then make a new one and thereby never generate any charge. So one would change postulates, yes, but only after cancelling (as-ising) the ones which one has adhered to so far and which have become unworkable. And one would do so on the basis of one's own volition, not because one has been persuaded or bullied into it. The end product would be "successfully accomplished survival".

At this point the reproach could be thrown in that such an attitude was egocentric and betrayed a weak character. That it meant changing direction like a flag in the wind. Egocentric it doesn't have to be – we will see why in the next chapter. A sign of a weak character it is not, as long as the person involved takes his bearings with reference to a high purpose and a broad game, and when he is determined to not go one fraction of a millimeter off it. Whoever lives along such lines may have to go through all manner of hardships, but he won't ever be a traitor to himself. – "Living by as-isness" therefore is by no means the same as the ill-reputed "way of the least resistence". In fact, these two principles don't even exclude, but actually complement each other! Water for example always goes the way of the least resistence, yet never loses sight of its main goal: it always reaches the ocean.

To continue with having committed the overt of betraying one's own certainty: the person doing so usually can't confront it. He does not want it known that it happened. He not-ises it for himself and he withholds it from others. It is not to be mentioned or brought up as it would endanger his survival. It's safer to keep it covered than to bring it out in the open.

Example: Fred is at Linda's party. Lots of people there. Fred spills a glas of red wine on the beige carpet. He is startled, helpless and thinks: "Oh no!" – which means as much as "I can't have done this; I can't have been that stupid; it wasn't me". Here then is the overt. He did something, knows he did, pretends he didn't, and pretends it not only to himself but to everybody else, too. So it's an overt in the first universe and in the third one, too. And his postulate of "Oh no" is of course the alter-is, i.e. the withhold he has from himself and from others regarding the truth of the matter.

Now Fred has a real problem. He has created a nice little Goals-Problems-Mass (GPM) for himself. He is torn between "should I tell – shouldn't I tell", "Was it me – no, it can't have been me". This problem keeps going around in his mind.

Consequently, Fred will avoid meeting the eyes of Linda for the rest of his time at the party, and he'll find a good reason to leave earlier than he would have otherwise. When he says goodbye to Linda he makes sure not to look straight at her. Linda says: "Nice you came, dear. I hope you liked the red wine." And she winks at him with one eye. Fred feels caught out. Does she know? Or doesn't she? His withhold has been restimulated and he wonders if Linda knows what he did. He can't tell. Hastily he goes off. His friendliness towards Linda is markedly lowered in the future. He avoids her as much as he can which isn't so easy as she works in the same office. His colleagues notice that there is something cooking and ask him about it. He drops scathing and critical remarks about Linda and makes her look a rather despicable person in order to have a "good reason" not to talk to her any more and to justify this before everybody else.

In technical terms, this is the sequence: overt leads to withhold leads to missed withhold leads to problem. When the withhold was almost found out to the point of one wondering if the other knows or not, we talk about a "missed withhold". A missed withhold is the act of another, of the one who is almost finding out; in our example it is Linda. The guilty party has the withhold; the other is knowingly or unknowingly doing or saying something which restimulates the withhold. But she doesn't hit it smack in the middle so that the sparks fly, she *misses* it. In this manner it may be restimulated forever after. The well-known phenomenon going along with it, is a bad conscience.

Now the person has a problem: who can he possibly trust? Do they know or don't they? Which of course leads to an "ARC-break", i.e. a lowering or even breaking of one's willingness to communicate with the other, share reality or have affinity with him or her. A typical indicator for a missed withhold is Fred complaining about Linda. The clever auditor would immediately ask: what has Fred done to Linda that he has to cover up by invalidating her?

These, then, are the **rudiments: overt, withhold, missed withhold, problem, ARC-Break**. The term "rudiment" implies that this is what life is basically composed of. When "the ruds are in" life is good fun, when "the ruds are out" there is some sort of undetected trouble afoot (as the auditor jargon has it).

MOTIVATORS AND SERVICE FACSIMILES

Now that we know what an overt is, we can go a step further and look at the **overt-motivator sequence**. A "motivator" is *"an aggressive or destructive act received by the person (. . .). It's called a motivator because it tends to prompt that one pays it back – it "motivates" a new overt"* [2].

Example: you lost the tennis match (motivator received), blame it on the racket, knock the racket against the wall in anger and break it. "Well-justified", certainly, but an overt against the poor tennis racket nevertheless. You original overt was not being able to have how badly you played – which made you lose the match. Or: Paul, at the age of 12, gets spanked by his father for having bad marks at school (motivator received). At the age of 35, Paul spanks his own son for having bad marks at school ("well-justified", of course).

As we have seen in the example of Fred at Linda's party: the motivator he received by the disastrous occurence of the wine glas spilling its wine (all by itself, naturally) gives Fred ample reason for snide comments and unjust "criticism" against Linda. ("Why doesn't she get herself a set of wine glasses which don't tip over so easily", etc.) He does it in an attempt to belittle the person he has committed the overt against, and make it look as if that person deserved it – all in the effort to make it all right that the carpet was messed up.

In scientologese this is called "being motivator hungry"; it serves to make oneself right. What do you do when you feel found out by someone and get a bad conscience? You claim that he did something terrible to you. You react in two ways: Either you attack him to wipe him out, be it socially, business-wise or even physically. Or you withdraw into the sulking depth of an ARC-break.

The interesting thing about it is the sequence: overt first, motivator second. It's not a motivator-overt sequence. Any "look-what-they've-done-to-me" attitude can be easily shattered by asking: "And what have *you* done that made it come about?" One had the responsibility to make it go right. One didn't, and got under the wheels. How come one didn't?

When one has been hit, claims to be a poor victim, and starts feeling terribly right whilst making others wrong, one has begun to use a **Service Facsimile**. *"Service because they serve him. Facsimile because they are in mental image picture form. They explain his disabilities as well. The facsimile part is actually a self-installed disability that "explains" how he is not responsible for being able* *to cope. So he is not wrong for not coping. Part of the "package" is to be right by making wrong. The service facsimile is therefore a picture containing an explanation of self condition and also a fixed method of making others wrong. (. . .) It is simply a time when you tried to do something and were hurt or failed and got sympathy for it. Then afterwards when you were hurt or failed and wanted an explanation, you used it. And if you didn't succeed in getting sympathy for it, you used it so hard it became a psychosomatic illness. (. . .) It's your explanation to yourself and the world as to how and why you failed. It once got you sympathy"* [2].

Example: little William, 5 years old, climbs up the ladder to the appletree. He misses a rung, stumbles and falls down. That's an overt, it's his fault; he should have watched out better. He is unconscious for a moment, comes to and feels nauseous. (This remains non-confronted so it is an engram.) He is put to bed immediately, taken care of, pampered; Aunt Mary scolds Uncle Peter for allowing "that poor little boy" to climb up this "terribly high" ladder. Little William knows to take an advantage when he sees one: Uncle Peter has to carry him upstairs to his bedroom every night now, because William "feels so weak at the sight of that high staircase". When Uncle Peter tells him he is a big boy and has already demonstrated that he *can* go upstairs by himself and maybe should try again now, William says he would really like to try but just now he feels so nauseous. So he gets carried up, particularly as Aunt Mary is all worried.

What William is doing here: he is consciously using the facsimile of the accident plus its physical sensation (the nausea) to keep up his victim position and thereby control his environment. The trick is that he pretends to be willing to co-operate but that he unfortunately can't because of a somatic he ("of course") is not in control of. So he pretends not to be able and expects others to coax him back into a state of being able, without ever doing them the favour.

This can go a long way. It will finally end up in a real psychosomatic illnes. All William has to do to "pull one in", is to use his

146

facsimile really hard, put lots of attention on it and restimulate the engram by his own efforts. (He *was* unconscious and *did* feel nauseous, after all. And as he never confronted it, it was recorded as an engram by the body and as a little GPM by him.)

Here is the further development: William, now 16 years old, has a school exam coming up. He has never studied up on this particular subject. The world looks black to him. The next week (exams) is going to be a disaster, he knows it already. These things are much too difficult for his little brain. He tells his mother that he is afraid. His mother tells him to sit down and learn. William sits down and – as a "solution" – faints (the unconsciousnes of the engram) and drops off the chair. He feels quite sick suddenly (the nausea of the engram). He has to stay in bed, feels weak, can't learn. Mother writes a note of excuse to the headmaster that her son can't attend the exams. Such a poor victim. Certainly he can't be expected to be responsible for his progress at school, what with that inexplicable and sudden illness.

And on it goes. In the final stage, at age 35, William will have developed a permanent stomach ulcer which gives him a good and generally acceptable reason not to appear in the office when more than the usual is being demanded. And it's a real ulcer; the doctor has diagnosed it so. Nobody would argue with that, given the usual social agreements on such matters.

By this time, anything will be explained by the ulcer, just anything. It's the most marvellously useful method of being irresponsible and bad-tempered without having to account for it. Its drawback is that William *genuinely* has become a victim now. What started out as a bit of boyish play-acting in an aberrated attempt to control others, turned into a "survival" mechanism, to an attitude of "must be right". Its original deliberateness was totally and utterly lost along the way. William can't drop his Service Facsimile any more. He *has* a psychosomatic illness now. It is the result of his attempt „*to make self right and others wrong, to dominate or escape domination and enhance own survival and injure that of others*" [2].

CONCLUSIONS

In view of the fundamental principle of "GPM = 1st postulate + 2nd postulate" it appears that the making of a 2nd postulate is *the* overt act to beget all later overt acts. It is at this point that the thetan violates his integrity. In order to cover this up, he will either claim to have received a motivator and therefore feel justified in committing "well-motivated" misdeeds, or he will use service facsimiles to dominate everybody and escape domination oneself. Both – motivators as well as "SerFacs" – go back to the 2nd postulate. They are a dramatization of the succumb- and victim-attitude inherent in any 2nd postulate. The difference between the two dramatizations lies in their position on the tone scale: someone using motivators, acts overtly antagonistic (2.0) or angry (1.5); someone using Ser-Facs acts on the sly. He is just above fear (1.0), yet below openly shown resentment (1.3), at a point called "covert hostility" (1.1).

Ethics and The Dynamics of Life

THE DYNAMICS

In the begining of the last chapter it was mentioned that "successfully accomplished survival" made one right for what one did in order to achieve one's purposes. We meant to come back to this, and we are doing so now. You might call it a very selfish attitude, and you would be right. Indeed, if it were understood on a strictly individual basis, I'd call it that way, too. Yet the above sentence is probably quite acceptable, if set in a wide enough supra-individual framework. This is provided by the eight **dynamics**.

The thetan, as a thought being, is in principle above all games. He is infinite and therefore static. This is the 8th dynamic. (How come it is called a "dynamic" when it in fact represents a static, will be explained in a minute.)

In order to play a game, the thetan has to firstly postulate one, secondly he has to enter the realm of duality by assuming a beingness, thirdly he has to act from a certain viewpoint. Once he has made himself a definite terminal, communication and all the phenomena of ARC are possible. –This is happening on the 7th dynamic.

Having started to work with attention units and dimension points (theta quanta), he of course creates mental mest now and forms agreements with regard to physical mest. This is the 6th dynamic, the dynamic of inorganic mest: rocks, chairs, houses, fluids, gases, planets, suns, galaxies. (Hubbard looks at physical mest in the same terms as mental mest: condensed and "frozen" theta quanta. Physical mest is just a little more solid than mental mest. Think of a diamond – good. Now squeeze real hard and have a genuine solid diamond in front of you – very good. If you could do that you'd be in excellent shape as a thetan.)

On the 5th dynamic, there are all forms of organic life: plants, animal and human bodies. They are run by Genetic Entities as

149

long as they are alive. Once they are dead, they are part of the 6th dynamic.

The bodies plus the thetans living "in" them are considered the 4th dynamic of a specific planet. 4th dynamic means: all the people on a particular planet.

People form groups in order to work, help each other out or play games together. – This is the 3rd dynamic.

To keep the human race going and provide bodies for one's own future, one needs to procreate. Sex, children, family – this is the 2nd dynamic (often abbreviated "2D").

One's own life in the body one happens to have, expressing oneself individually by means of hobbies, sports, artistic activities, whatever – that is the 1st dynamic.

These dynamics overlap, certainly. There is not one act in life where the full set of dynamics wouldn't come to bear – one may be more emphasized than the other, yes, but they are all there. Example: you, the thetan (8th dynamic), sit in the office in your identity as secretary (7th dynamic), and need some coffee (6th dynamic), to satisfy the thirst of your body (5th dynamic). The office staff (3rd dynamic) have put money together to buy a coffee machine (6th dynamic). Getting the coffee from Brazil to Brighton was an operation involving half the people on the planet (4th dynamic). You use the cup your husband gave you as a present once (2nd dynamic). You make a cup of coffee for yourself and enjoy it (1st dynamic).

Usually, dynamics are looked at as "survival urges" covering an ever expanding range. Here you start at the bottom with the 1st dynamic and count upwards: There is the urge to survive as yourself, as your family, as your group, as mankind, as a healthy natural environment, as a planet, as a spirit, and as an infinite being. The *urge* to survive as infinity makes the 8th dynamic a "dynamic".

In order to grow along the dynamics one must have accomplished stability on a certain dynamic before approaching the next one. The power to operate on the next higher dynamic is derived from standing on the solid platform of the dynamics below it. If, for example, the President of the United States, whose decisions surely influence the fate of the 4th dynamic, wasn't backed up by the 3rd dynamic of his aids and the American people, if he were having family trouble (2nd dynamic), if he had a case problem and needed therapy (1st dynamic), his attention would get pulled down from the 4th dynamic to lower dynamics. He would have to fix the emergency and danger situations on the lower dynamics before being able to resume his operations on the 4th dynamic. To that extent, his post would have been left unattended to. So a danger situation was brought about on a higher dynamic because of weak spots on lower dynamics.

ETHICS AND MORALS

Going back to "successfully accomplished survival" making one right for what one did: The attitude connected with this phrase is not selfish if it is proven to occur on a higher dynamic than the first. Suddenly we find ourselves engaged in a discussion of ethics! Hubbard's concept of ethics is built around the term **optimum solution**. An optimum solution is always to be sought by the decision maker. He is to make sure that – to the best of his knowledge – the survival of the maximum number of terminals involved in his decision is furthered by his decision. Only the minimum number of terminals is to be inhibited in their survival.

Dn Ax.192: "Optimum survival behaviour consists of effort in the maximum survival interest in everything concerned in the dynamics."
Ax.193: "The optimum survival solution of any problem would consists of the highest attainable survival for every dynamic concerned" [1].

This requires great flexibility on the side of the decision maker (thetan) as his decisions have to always be made "here and now". He can't think today as he thought only yesterday as yesterday's situation is not the same as today's. Many variables may have changed overnight and therefore the whole thing must be thought over again. Not only his flexibility but as well the number of dynamics a person can think on determine his chances for success. Example: a company owner who can only think on the 1st and 2nd dynamic, will exploit the company for his personal welfare and that of his family. He won't care in the least for the life of his workers as he is not interested in them, but in profit alone. This attitude is shortsighted as it leads to a lot of trouble for his personnel department: many sick leaves, frequent staff changes. In the end the quality and quantity of production will suffer. If this company owner were able to think on the 3rd dynamic he would consider the welfare of all concerned when he makes his decisions, i.e. his own, that of his family *and* that of his workers. If he were, beyond this, capable of thinking on the 4th dynamic he would take care not to produce things which might damage mankind on the whole – simply because in the end it would damage him. And so on, up the dynamics. He thinks of his own survival in terms of everybody's survival, because he knows that he is not alone in the world. When he knows, too, that he will be born again and will have to clean up the mess he made this lifetime in his next lifetime, he will think twice of making contrasurvival decisions.

The more higher dynamics someone can incorporate in his thinking, the higher is – according to Hubbard – his **potential value**. When his decisions are *as well* aligned with an optimum solution, not only his potential value but his actual **worth**, too, will be high. However, if his decisions are not aligned in such manner, such a person – because of his very intelligence with regard to higher dynamics – is likely to be extremely destructive. As is only all too often demonstrated in politics and history. (As a reference to this, see "The Fundamental Axioms of Dianetics" in DMSMH or in [1].)

Traditional morals are only one factor to be considered in an ethical decision. An ethical decision tries to find a solution which guarantees the optimum survival for all concerned. There are situations where it is saner, more pro-survival and therefore more ethical, to act *against* traditional morals. By some individuals doing so, a whole society may change. Look at the arguments for and against marriage between catholics and protestants, about premarital sex, abortion, single parents bringing up their children, homosexuality, and look how the pertinent values have changed since the beginning of this century. General morals are changed by the disagreement of individuals who look for new and ethical solutions.

For the sake of completion it must unfortunately be added that morals are as well subjected to change, because certain individuals manage to propagate their unethical solutions by means of large-scale media campaigns. In this manner, suppressive powers succeed in steering society to the point where they want to have it [7, 8, 9, 10]. Whoever controls the communication lines on the 4th dynamic, determines the reality of people, i.e their moral judgement – and thereby the affinity of one nation with the other.

What do ethics matters have to do with auditing? Well, a lot. Simply because all overts start with the untruth of a 2nd postulate masking the truth of a 1st postulate. This is the charge which reads on the meter. And this is what the auditor is concerned with. He is *not* concerned with the value systems and beliefs of the pc. He is only looking for disagreements the pc has with himself, inside his own universe. He is looking for cracks in the pc's personal integrity. It would be against his code if he were passing evaluative judgements on the pc's life and standards of behaviour.

The pc has his very personal principles. He is certain of their truth and value. As well, he is sworn in to the laws and morals of his chosen group and makes them his own. Someone else may consider the pc's group insane and murderous, but he, the pc, is certain that this group deserves his support. He will develop charge anytime he transgresses against his own laws or against those he absorbed from his group. This, to him, is unethical. Supposing he were a hunter and transgressed against the codes and customs of hunting, he'd feel guilty. But the subject of killing animals as such will never come up in his sessions! Because he has no disagreements whatsoever with the killing part of hunting. The next pc, who is a vegetarian, transgressed his own principles when he ate a steak the other day. He had to; it was his grandmother's birthday; she would have been very hurt had he said "no" to her steak. But he feels guilty; he feels that he has contributed to the demand for steaks and thereby to the continuation of cows being killed. He lives within a different set of agreements than the hunter; accordingly he has charge on quite different items.

It follows that the auditor works "inside" the pc's universe and inside his ethics frame of reference. The vegetarian has charge on eating steaks – fine, it'll be handled in his next sesion. The hunter likes his steaks – fine, no need to mention it any further.

COMPETENCE

There are moments when it is more important to do an ethics consultation than to just carry on auditing. This is not done as part of a session but as a separate cycle, preferably by a different person than the auditor.

Anyone making a mistake through incompetence naturally builds up charge because of it. He wanted the best and fouled it all up and now he is upset. Auditing takes this charge away. But auditing does not increase the person's competence! In order to increase his competence, the person would have to study and learn so that he may control things better and bear higher responsibility regarding them.

All auditing deals with the removal of charge. This is called **negative gain**. The pc wins by losing a burden. Positive gain would be achieved by studying, and by living one's life on a high level of awareness and ethics. Removal of charge alone may make a Clear but it doesn't necessarily make a fellow who is useful to have around. As Hubbard puts it in the parable of the cleared cannibal: *"The individual without engrams seeks survi-*

val along all of the dynamics in accordance with his breadth of understanding. This does not mean that a Zulu who has been cleared of all his engrams would not continue to eat missionaries if he were a cannibal by education; but it does mean that he would be as rational as possible about eating missionaries; further, it would be easier to re-educate him about eating missionaries if he were a Clear" [2]. When we wish to increase knowledge, responsibility or control, we are encountering an interrelationship similar to that of the ARC-triangle: the **KRC-triangle**. Its three components knowledge, responsibility and control (KRC) amount to competence.

Knowledge consists of the complete store of experience a person has available to draw from. **Responsibility** is expressed in the willingness to predict a result and to bear the consequences of success and failure. **Control** is simply defined as the ability to start, change and stop things, people or activities. Control makes prediction possible.

As pointed out above, there is an interrelationship between these three components. In order to increase a person's control you must increase his knowledge and give him more responsibility. Conversely: if someone has vast knowledge and no responsibility, his activities will run out of control.

Examples: whoever operates the trigger of an atomic weapon, controls a terrifying devastation potential and therefore bears a gigantic responsibility; he can only live up to it if he knows what he is dealing with and what the consequences are. Someone who knows that tipping old engine oil down a drainpipe leads to water pollution, automatically has the responsibility to not do that, but get rid of his wastes in a controlled way. A senior who is responsible for his production and a number of juniors, must have great knowledge of his job in order to predict, supervise and control all activities.

Competence and incompetence are solely determined by the degree of knowledge, responsibility and control demonstrated by a person with regard to a certain activity. Competence and incompetence can be unequivocally told by looking at someone's products. They are expressed in deeds not words.

ARC and KRC are not two separate systems but mutually dependent. Example: the science of physics provides the means to build surgical lasers on the one hand and atom bombs on the other hand. What is being done, depends on the KRC of the physicist and on his ARC with mankind. It's not the fault of physics when cities get bombed but that of the man who built the bombs. Yes, you may argue, but wasn't he very competent, too? Because his bombs went off at the right moment, didn't they? True. So he was competent. But then his ARC regarding the dynamics involved was very low. He had high responsibility for his bombs but low affinity for who was going to get killed by them. He didn't care about that. So you show him some pictures of people blown up by his bombs. Now that he knows what effect he is causing, now that this reality entered his mind, he may change his attitude and join the Peace Corps. If he *has* the reality but he still doesn't care, there must be something below it. It's the quality of the person's intention. *"Insanity is the overt or covert but always complex and continous determination to harm or destroy"* [17]. When a thetan is biased in such a way he will have a lot of affinity with dead bodies and be very responsible to produce a lot of them. Such person is called a **suppressive person (SP)**. (He can be handled by auditing. It takes a lot of work, though – if he wants it at all! SPs usually don't volunteer to change their ways and get better.)

Going back to the interdependence between ARC and KRC: in the more usual (sane instead of insane) run of life, ARC alone does not suffice to make it; it takes KRC as well. Love without competence may not get anyone anywhere, but it surely "feels nice". Competence without any friendliness and understanding (as expressed in a dictatorial mentality) gets things done all right – but only temporarily as the hate accumulated by those this sort of competence is enforced on, will be its final stumbling block.

ARC and KRC, understanding and competence, go best hand in hand. For this reason they have been chosen by Hubbard to form the scientology symbol: two triangles with an S weaving through them. The interesting thing about it is that the KRC-triangle is the upper triangle. *"Little by little one can make anything go right by: increasing KNOWLEDGE on all dynamics, increasing RESPONSIBILITY on all dynamics, increasing CONTROL on all dynamics"* [2].

Gradients of Clearing

A THEORY OF THE BRIDGE

Having examined these different explanatory models on the subject of thetan-mind-body, we are finally in a position to answer the question: What is auditing?

It is a procedure which reduces charge by encouraging the individual to look at his past, present and future, to confront the games conditions he has created by his postulates and considerations, to dissolve them and the ridges which go along with them and come out more self-determined than before. He was being the effect of all this; now he is at cause over it. He can run his life better. The gradient steps needed to get to this point Hubbard calls a "bridge". *"BRIDGE, THE, 2. A term originating in early Dianetic days to symbolize travel from unknowingness to revelation"* [2].

For a description of the bridge, the Factors and Axioms are most useful. First, the way downward: anytime a thetan decides to cause an effect (Fac. 1), he has to assume a beingness, (Fac. 2) and then do something (Fac. 3-7) in order to have something (Fac. 10). The more thetans are involved in this, the more complex this game will become (Fac. 11-23). Things get bad for our thetan when he starts considering that his dimension points are too valuable to be lost or given up. He introverts into what he has already created and invalidates his knowledge that he can create more of them. Suddenly there is scarcity; he thinks because his creations can perish he might perish, too, and starts to think of death (Fac. 24, 25). Now he believes that he "must become" someone and forgets that he already is someone anyway (Fac. 27). He has invalidated his own true nature as a thetan.

How can he pull himself back up? – By sorting out the mess bit by bit, exactly as described in Factor 28. The exact rules to be followed are given in the Axioms: he separates his 1st postulates from his 2nd postulates (Ax. 36) by confronting the not-isnesses and alter-isnesses (Ax. 11) and as-ises them by the use of ARC (Ax. 24). Eventually he will wind up back at the top: before the begining (Fac. 1), as a static (Axiom 1). – He has worked himself out of this particular game and can start a new one by assuming a new beingness (Fac. 2).

So what is a bridge? – It's the journey of a thetan from a state of identification with masses and the corresponding "unknowingness", to the "revelation" of having a static quality above and beyond mest. He gets there by rehabilitating his ability to have or not have masses at will [20]. This does not mean that he would stop being a player of games. But it does mean the end of his unawareness and his entanglement in mest.

When one has completed one's case, one would not be fixated on one's first universe problems and masses but be extraverted and find one's games and problems in the third universe. At this stage one could not have further casegain through auditing (as there isn't any case left), but would have one's gains in life by the application of ethics, tech and admin know-how. One would demonstrate competence *observably*, i.e. in the third universe (Dn Ax. 194).

The end result, in the words of Hubbard: *"A qualitative return of confidence in self, not quantitative handling of bank."* (HCOB 7.4.60). *"Certainty in all three universes (. . .)."* (Fac. 28). *"A person who is at cause over his own reactive bank and can create and uncreate it at will"* (Ability, March 59). *"He finally winds up without a reactive bank and he's happy about it because he can mock one up anytime he wants, but he doesn't have to now. (. . .) It's a horrible truth that people – through irresponsibility – mocked up all of their own difficulties"* (Clearing Congress 1958, video tape 6).

How much bridge does it take to perform such a rehabilitation to its end phenomenon? – This is different from person to person. It depends on how much the thetan actually considers himself identified with masses.

CLEAR AND OT – SEEN HISTORICALLY

When Hubbard originally formulated the sentences above, he was referring to the state of Clear. We are saying, though, that the end of the bridge is "Case Completion" rather than "Clear". So what does that mean? And what happened to the much-rumoured "OT"?

With these questions we wind up right in the middle of the confusion of terms and concepts regarding this subject. What does Clear really mean? And OT? This is hard to answer in one word, because there has been a confusing number of definitions of Clear between 1950 and 1978 and a change in the definition of "reactive bank". The definition of "OT" became increasingly shallow. It is not easy to find one's way through this, but we may at least try. (This is not a "merely historical" easy, by the way, but a very practical one: because without a goal you can't guide, and guiding is the auditor's task; so he must know his goal.)

Let us take an unhurried look, then, at the development of the concepts in question. In "Dianetics" we find: *"A clear (noun) is an individual who, as a result of dianetic therapy, has neither active nor potential psycho-somatic illness or aberration"* (p. 170). *"There are no demon circuits in his mind (. . .)"* (p. 171). *"In a clear, the entire content* (of the reactive bank) *is removed"* (p. 174). *"Cells, not the individual, are evidenced to record pain. And the reactive engram bank is composed only of cells. (. . .) The engram is not a memory; it is a cellular trace of recordings impinged deeply into the very structure of the body itself"* (p. 128). – This is how Hubbard sees the **Clear** and the reactive bank in 1950. The thetan does not exist under this name yet. He is called "I" or "basic personality". The thetan himself does not make pictures; they press in on him from the body only and impede his natural rationality.

"History of Man" (1952, abbreviated HOM), "Scientology 8-8008" (1953, abbr. 8-8008) and "Creation of Human Ability" (1954, abbr. COHA) all circle around the same thought: how does one manage to make the thetan come out of his body? Since HOM the thetan exists under this name. As the result of dianetic therapy he has become a "Mest Clear" and sticks to his body as if glued in. Apart from **Mest Clear** he is as well called **Homo Novis**. What's wrong with him? *"This homo novis is limited in his self-determinism by all the economic and social restrictions of an aberrated society. He is not free of food, clothing or shelter. He dies when you get him too cold, he perishes when the oxygen content drops too low. He is living in a tolerance band which keeps him cramped to the face of one second-rate planet in a tenth-rate system, prey to all the ill will that blows. Is this being free and self-determined?"* (HOM, p. 38.) Therefore the motto: *"The goal (. . .) is OPERATING THETAN, a higher goal than earlier procedures."* (8-8008, p. 115.)

This higher goal is called **Theta Clear**: *"A being who is reasonably stable outside the body (. . .)."* (8-8008, Glossary.) Above that there is yet another higher goal, the **Cleared Theta Clear**: *"A person (. . .) who is able to create illusions perceivable by others at will, to handle MEST universe objects without mechanical means and to have and feel no need of bodies or even the MEST universe to keep himself and his friends interested in existence."* (8-8008, p. 114.)

In order to attain these things it seemed advisable to catapult the thetan out of his body instead of auditing a sheer endless quantity of entities one by one. *"These entities run off their own past deaths, on other tracks (. . .). They are actually the basis of "demon circuits" (as covered in DIANETICS: THE MODERN SCIENCE OF MENTAL HEALTH) (. . .)."* (HOM, p. 14.) *"The THETA BEING is the principal target of the auditor. (. . .) The main thing wrong with any preclear is that he cannot disentangle himself from entities and somatic entities, from demon circuits and mest bodies."* (HOM, p. 37.)

Now, in contrast to the days of "Dianetics", the focus of attention was on the thetan himself. Hubbard names four approaches for solving a case. The last one deals with the timetrack of the thetan-plus-beingness, i.e. with someone who has a wavelength, self-created automatisms and a position in space. *"Of the four only the last is actually capable of producing the clear with any rapidity."* (HOM, p. 9.) The timetrack of "Dianetics", restricted to the present life, had become extended trillions of years into a past when very thorough and lasting implants were dealt out and taken in. Now the thetan's *own* pictures were starting to be looked at – which is not done at all in "Dianetics". Accordingly, the reactive bank was not described as a mere cellular affair any more, but as *"the ridge automatic response system"*. The "somatic mind" became the *"genetic entity plus the brain system of the body"*. (Both quotes from 8-8008, glossary.)

As we saw above: Hubbard tried to achieve exteriorizations by "going past the entities". This did not always work well for those who took part in the experiment, the circle closest to Hubbard. Amazing things were made to happen, feats which came very close to the states mentioned above – yet unfortunately the participants did not survive it in some cases! Their entities became restimulated to such extent that their bodies broke down under the strain and died. (This was reported by one of the then – and since re-incarnated – students.)

The whole track with its implants increasingly constituted a problem. Hubbard sat down for quite a while to study GPMs, particularly in the early 60's. The reactive mind was more and more seen as connected to implants and GPMs. 1965 the bridge was arranged in a new and different way. It consisted of five "release grades". What previously was called Mest-Clear or Dianetic-Clear is now called "Second Stage Release". The "real" Clear is the **Scientology Clear**, the "Fifth Stage Release". Similar to "Dianetics", the claim is raised that *"one has to have run out the whole remaining reactive mind."* (See "Stages of Release" in the Tech Dict.) The section of the reactive mind handled here became known as the R6-bank, because it was worked on with an auditing process called Routine 6. The Pre-Clear audited for hundreds of hours on the content of an implant which was assumed to have happened to him only (not his entities), and which was called the "Clearing Course Implant". It's all on his own track. He audits "solo". Solo-auditing was a novelty then: the auditor has the two cans (insulated from each other) in one hand, and with the other he operates the E-meter and writes down the session actions.

Even after 1965 Clears showed to be susceptible to aberrations and psychosomatic illnesses. Evidently there was – at long last – no way around dealing with the so far neglected entities. And this is how the OT levels I-III were developed, which since 1967 became a fixed part of the bridge.

Hubbard had to give his Clears the reality of what Xenu had done, 75 million years ago, as they didn't find out by themselves. *He* could confront and do the research about it; *they* couldn't. So he had to tell them. Once a Clear is informed about this OT III reality, he can get in communication with the pertinent ridges and develop enough affinity to "blow" (as-is) them.

If it weren't for the particular complexity of the OT III ridges, a Clear could be expected to clean them up simply by direct confront. Yet OT III, being designed not to be found out about, does not permit this approach. So Hubbard said: "Look, there's some more case, and it's on the 3rd and 4th dynamic. It may not have happened to all of you personally (back then) but you surely went into contact with it from the day you started taking a position on Earth. It's weighing you down and you don't even know it. So look at these materials and start doing something about it. As-ising these ridges will not only free you but clean the air for this planet, too. And it will wreck the game of Xenu, and that's what we want." – Well, since people *had* the next section of case and were now informed about its contents, they could of course sit down with their solo-cans, confront it, increase their ARC and havingnes concerning it and as-is it. OT III was extremely successful; enormous wins and visible changes of body and personality went along with it as a rule.

That it was only in 1965, after the release of Clear, that Hubbard should have started to see that Xenu was in his way, is for two reasons unlikely: Firstly there is the 1963 policy quoted in

Part One, where Hubbard says that Clear and Theta Clear were not any more the course to take, but that the making of OTs had priority because there was a battle to be fought. Secondly, the Clearing Course Implant from about roughly one quadrillion years ago, which had apparently meant the end of being Clear, is in terms of content closely related to the implant from 75 million years ago. In both Xenu was the stage manager. From this one may conclude that Hubbard, from 1963 onwards, had started developing the bridge according to strategic and not technical priorities.

The bridge used since 1970 does look like it. Apart from some minor changes it is still in use nowadays – at least in the CofS – and prescribes the route to take. A number of dianetics and scientology processes lead up to the state of Clear which is for the first time seen as limited to the 1st dynamic: *"A thetan who can be at cause knowingly and at will over mental matter, energy, space and time as regards the first dynamic"* [2]. Then follow OT I-III where disturbing influences (ridges and entities) on the 3rd and 4th dynamic are eliminated.

This would actually result in something like a "complete Clear" – but it isn't anywhere stated that way. However, it is suggested in two ways: Firstly, Hubbard recommends as the last step on OT III that one should look along one's own track – after having cleaned up all entities – and check into one's own involvement 75 million years ago, be it on the overt or on the motivator side.

So there could be still charge on one's *own* time track! Which of course should not be the case when one takes the definition of "Clear on the first dynamic" literally. Which means that, with Clear, it is *not* all over yet. Secondly, the original levels above OT III, OT IV-VII, contained exercises concerning exteriorisation. These levels therefore constitute an attempt to attain what always had been attempted after Clear: the stably exteriorized thetan, once called "Theta Clear". And above that, one step higher, there is OT VIII as a vision: *"OPERATING THETAN, OT VIII: Ability to be at cause knowingly and at will over thought, life, form, matter, energy, space and time, subjective and objective"* [1]. Which is nothing else but the Cleared Theta Clear postulated already 17 years earlier – unattained then as well as today (1990). Neither then nor now are there the necessary auditing procedures in a finalized version.

Hubbard died without having reached his great goal. He was worn out by the problem of how to bring about at least as much as a clean and decent Clear under the bank-conditions of this planet. It therefore isn't a mere coincidence that his last word concerning the bridge refers to the composite case. In the bulletin "Nature of a Being" (1980) he says unequivocally that the thetan, apart form having his own bank, is surrounded by all sorts of entities, and that these obey the same laws as the thetan himself. Although he let a cat out of its bag a second time – marvelled at by the auditor community – which in fact had been out of the bag with "History of Man" once before, he used a slightly different tone this time: back in the past he had tried to find his way around the entities, now he cannot help including them. Whoever manages to handle the composite case in its totality, is a Clear in the full sense of the word; that is the message.

The changes which were made since 1978 regarding the bridge, must be understood in this context. The OT levels IV-VII were an attempt to fulfill the promise of Theta Clear and stable exteriorisation but didn't hold up to it. As well it became increasingly clear that even OT III was not enough to do away with all the entities whirling around the thetan. People either were not aware of them and became aberrated without knowing, or they – as auditors – could not handle them. Consequently the old exteriorisation-levels IV-VII were taken off the bridge in 1978, to become replaced by a set of "anti-entity" OT-levels. These became known under the name of "New Era Dianetics for OTs", abbreviated **NOTs**.

During this time (1978) there was as well the recognition that some people are naturally Clear on the 1st dynamic. They don't bring in much of a case from the start. This was called **Natural**

Clear by Hubbard. Of equally great importance was the realization that one can go Clear even through dianetic auditing. Whoever had, in the years before, completed his dianetic case and found no more engrams, was allowed to attest to **Dianetic Clear** – but he still had to audit his way through the series of implants of the Clearing Course in order to become **Scientology Clear**. This led to enourmous session difficulties, because one was trying to audit something where there was actually nothing. Many people gave up because of frustration or because they ran out of money. The message "the Dianetic Clear is a valid Clear" caused a sigh of relief around the world and got many going again who had got stuck on the lower bridge. This released a whole wave of power on to OT III – which of course was perfectly in accordance with Hubbard's plans. (For references see Tech Vol. XII.)

NOTs (1978) proved to be fairly ineffective, which was probably due to the people administering it rather than to Hubbard's concepts. Most NOTs bulletins were not actually written by Hubbard himself but by the leading tech man of the day, David Mayo. That they were signed "L. Ron Hubbard" was the done thing at the time. To what extent Hubbard was still in control and able to influence things, is an open question. As you may remember, he disappeared from the stage only a few years later.

After the initial hooray and clamorous worldwide marketing of NOTs as the fast route to real OT, it soon showed that there was no end to the auditing on this level. Some auditors worked for thousands (!) of hours on it, until in the end they got the feeling that the case was endless and disappointedly gave up. (Which didn't change the hooray and the marketing strategies of the CofS one bit.)

1982 the NOTs materials got into the hands of Bill Robertson who, during the great purge of 1982, had been thrown out of the CofS as a "suppressive person". After sixteen years of personal contact with Hubbard, Robertson was more familiar with his ways of working and thinking than anyone else. He turned the NOTs process into what it was originally intended for: namely to erase all aspects of foreign-made and enforced mental masses and energies, and to enable the thetan to be cause over them. This development of his, Robertson called "Excalibur" – after the legendary and lost book Hubbard allegedly had written in the thirties.

CONTEMPORARY DEFINITIONS

So much for the history of Clear and OT. What are we left with considering this confusion of terms? With the sobering realization that the OT-levels, NOTs and Excalibur amount to not more than a nicely rounded-off Clear – not just on the 1st dynamic, though, but as well on the 3rd and 4th. Why? Well, "Clear", because he can handle mental mest; "3rd and 4th dynamic" because it may not be made by himself only (1st dynamic), but as well by others (3rd dynamic), particularly at times of galactic upheavals (4th dynamic).

The unfortunate thing about it is that no term of the traditional scientology vocabulary covers this state correctly: "Mest Clear" does not fit because it refers to this lifetime only by definition; the "Dianetic-book Clear" it is not because that would imply a release from the aberrations of the GE (which belongs on the 5th dynamic); the "1965 Scientology Clear" is incorrect, too, insofar it refers to one's own timetrack only (1st dynamic); "OT" is not right because it was always booked for the ability to exteriorize. None of this fits exactly, yet there is something in all of them. At the end of the current bridge there is, as it were, a "Mest Clear on the dynamics 1, 3 and 4 with an individually different ability to exteriorize."

Which is not to say that it all comes down to nothing! Quite the contrary – it is a fabulous result! Anyone who has attained that state knows what I am talking about. One might characterize it more or less by the following: you know that you are an immortal spiritual being which exists independently of its current body; you act on a physical as well as a theta level and are aware of your own concurrent infinity; you are not particularly impressed by mental mest no matter of what origin; you are in good communication with your body and can audit and discharge the Genetic Entity; you perceive mental messages from animals, plants or bodyless thetans – in a word: you are in very good communication. Looking at it this way, we are not only dealing with a cleared-ness on the dynamics mentioned (1st, 3rd, 4th), but with a phenomenon covering other dynamics as well – for example the 5th and the 7th. How far this goes, is different from person to person. It can certainly be expanded on. It is stable on the dynamics 1, 3 and 4, on the others it is not (at this time). Therefore the concept of "clearing along the dynamics" offers itself as the next step to take.

The word "unfortunate" used above, solely refers to the circumstance that the OT-ness implied in the word "OT-level" does not set in to the expected extent. True, telepathic abilites increase throughout the OT-levels – if they did not, one could not possibly audit entities, let alone the "bad guys" in spaceships or implant stations. Except that these abilities come into play only when the charge of the solo-auditor pulls his attention in the direction of the bad guy. Once the solo-auditor has undone the control-line from the opposing thetan to himself, his telepathic perception of him usually disappears – at least with most solo-auditors it is so. The ability, arisen out of necessity, is not always available afterwards when it would be useful, particularly for "civilian purposes". Some have more talent there than others, and exercises always help – but still: the free-roaming thetan exterior cannot be claimed to be a predictable result of present-day scientology. It hasn't got as far as that yet. Theta Clear, therefore, still stands as a research project.
What are the consequences of our discussion for the practical work of the auditor in his session? Very important ones, because they make it possible to find the common denominator in Hubbard's thirty-year research, and to clarify the words "Clear" and "OT" once and forever. Result: a clear-cut course.

Here then is the common denominator: A **Clear** is a thetan who does not *react* any more. An **OT** is a thetan who *acts*, and does so solely by the strength and clarity of his postulates. (To what extent he is able to do this whilst being exterior and without using physical or mechanical means, is a matter of individual ability and does not enter this definition.)

Seen like this, any thetan is OT to a degree. But not every OT is necessarily a Clear! These are two separate categories of ability. A Clear won't be touched any more by mental mest; he is cause over it as long as he can recognize and dissolve it. An OT, however, may be aberrated in many ways, but has "incidentally", "from the moment of his birth" or through special training a number of abilities which make the rest of us gape in awe and wonder – such as telepathic healing, levitating, aura reading, fortune telling, bending or moving heavy metal objects, etc. The existence of such phenomena has been documented too widely in east and west as to allow an argument about them [21, 22, 23]. Despite all the universities of this world, nobody can explain them "scientifically" yet. Hubbard's philosophy at least offers an approach to an explanation – but cannot purport to *predictably* lead to such results.

Each auditor knows what spectacular things may happen as a result of a session. But each auditor knows as well how short the duration of such things may be. Of what binding agreements the pc disconnects when he comes in the possession of such abilities, is not always known. If it were, one could rehabilitate them case for case. At least, though, one can be sure that these abilities *exist*. And abilities, no matter what kind, *can* be rehabilitated by means of the tech. At this time, the correct angle of approach is not known yet. And this is where the task for the future lies.

One question has not been answered yet: When would someone be allowed to call himself Clear? To give a very pragmatic answer: When he can confront the remainder of his case and can audit it solo, without the need of another auditor. Which presupposes that he has achieved the following with the auditor's help: Firstly he has done away with his own case. Secondly he has got rid of all entities which he could contact by means of his natural awareness at the time of the auditing. (Some have a lot to do here, others very little.) If he still had these influencing factors, he would not be able to audit solo, because the entities of the composite case would restimulate his own ridges so vehemently that the cans would drop from his hands.

Below Clear, there is the well-known rule: "Auditor plus pc is greater than the bank". From Clear on it goes: "Solo-auditor plus tech is greater than the bank". A Clear, therefore, would be somebody who can go it alone up to case completion. His Clear-ness would extend to the 1st dynamic plus to such entities (3rd dynamic) which he can approach without additional restimulation. "Clear" means that he stays cause over it, that he can handle it when he gets touched by it. (When we use the word Clear further on in this text, it is to be understood in this definition.)

A **Case Completion** would be someone like a "full Clear with rudimentary OT abilities". Someone who would not *react* anymore and to some extent could *act* as an OT, on any given dynamic. This is a relative concept as a Case Completion would always depend on the state of the tech at the time. Currently a Case Completion refers to the dynamics 1, 3 and 4, as we have seen. The 5th dynamic by and large is still a terra incognita. (Words in **bold italics** refer to newly-coined terms and cannot be found in the Tech Dict.)

To what extent a Case Completion would be able to resist the **Between-Life Implants**, mentioned variously by Hubbard, is as yet an open question. Case Completions have been made during the last very few years only; none of them has so far dropped his body. So we will have to wait for at least twenty or thirty years before they would drop back in (voluntarily) and tell us what happened to them. (When *none of them* came back – that would be a good sign!) Regarding the Clears and OTs of the fifties and sixties who have made their "comeback", one can observe that they quite easily recall their past lives and their past scientological activities – it takes only a very few auditing hours. Which means nothing else than that they have become victims of the between-life implants as well, albeit to a lesser extent than *pre*-Clears.

One should not imagine the between-life implants being executed by implanter thetans who, equipped with butterfly nets, sneak around the planet waiting to catch a thetan as he tries to exteriorize after his death. These implants much rather come in the form of a firmly installed "electric cow fence" around Earth, consisting of a very fine field of vibrations which give the thetan a good jolt as soon as he approaches this frequency in the attempt to shake off his masses and thereby lose his ties to Earth. It is a one-way fence, by the way. It lets you in, but not out. In this field, too, a lot of research work has yet to be done.

FUTURE PROJECTS

Let us have a tentative look, then, at the possibility of "clearing along the dynamics": a **Clear on the 5th dynamic** would be in excellent contact with his GE and audit it when it demonstrates an aberration – he may even de-aberrate it entirely. He would be able to communicate with his cells; cancer and AIDS would not threaten him. However, the experiences made with the scientologists of the past twenty years have shown one unfortunate thing very clearly: the Clear on dynamics 1, 3 and 4 can quite comfortably live *alongside* his body, not *with* his body as he should do. He – the thetan – does not feel impeded by the body having a stomach ache, a skin disease or diabetes. When you audit such a person you will sooner or later get to the end phenomenon of him confronting his illness with full Havingness, and him feeling just fine – as a thetan – despite the illness. In most cases the next step cannot be taken, which is to receive the communications of the organs in trouble and audit them. (It ought to be emphasized again that the respective talents vary from person to person.) In this context it is quite interesting to note that the GE can be addressed by acupuncture, homeopathy, Bach Flower Remedies and hypnosis – with the thetan simply being left out of the procedure! How come he cannot achieve by himself, by direct communication, what the treatments above achieve in the GE, by the use of their respective means?

The Clear on the 5th dynamic implies the ***Clear on the 2nd dynamic***. Body and sexuality are **one** package, because both are governed by the GE – and sometimes by its aberrations. The 2nd dynamic probably is the most aberrated of them all. There is a lot left to clear up on it! Why for example does a sexually neutral thetan behave like a man or a woman as soon as he has taken the respective body? And how come he behaves the opposite way in the case of homosexuality? And where does the imaginetiveness of torturers come from, which is always directed towards the maiming of sexual organs? It all comes from the GE. The OT III implants do not suffice as an explanation. It is earlier on the timetrack.

A thetan who uses a body whilst being free of the aberrating influences of the GE – that would be a Clear in the full sense of "Dianetics". Would it be a **Theta Clear**, too? Could it be possible that one's ability to stably exteriorize are blocked by ages-old agreements with the GE? By so far undetected implants? Hubbard, in 1952, had tried to obtain a **One-shot Clear**. He used key-out processes which directly aim at exteriorization. This approach failed. And up to this day it has not been found out what the compulsion to interiorize is based on. Back in the 50s, the fast scientology-style key-out approach did not do the trick – perhaps the slow methods of dianetics would lead to success? By handling and erasing all the engrams of the GE?

The next step upwards would be the ***Clear on the 6th dynamic***. He could not be disturbed by the vibrations of rocks or water veins, by X-rays or whatever inorganic radiation source. He could locate it and de-aberrate it by auditing, if it were aberrated; at least he could keep it from influencing his body or

173

himself. – Let us imagine a thetan for a moment, who would understand mest completely and utterly, who could communicate with each minute subatomic particle lovingly – would he not, as the next step, begin to influence mest causatively? By making it storm and snow on a bright sunny day, by making stones melt, by moving mountains? By creating solid objects out of nothing or letting his body pass through walls? Is it here where we find the **Cleared Theta Clear**?

A Clear on the 7th dynamic should be able to voluntarily pick up any affinity vibration, any postulate crossing his own game, any type of theta communication with the same clarity as a radio receives the wave frequencies of a broadcasting station. No matter if he encountered the spirits of plants and mountains or the enticing calls of bodyless thetans from other universes – neither of them would manage to overwhelm him, subjugate his will and subtly guide him. Such attempts would glance off his alertness. He would even go one step further and audit the senders of such messages, should they be of unethical nature. *"The price of freedom: constant alertness, constant willingness to fight back. There is no other price."* [2]
It is doubtful if such a thetan were still to be met in the physical universe. He would probably not be bothered with mest-related activities any longer. He would be a "pure beingness" (Fac. 2) but have no location (Fac. 3). This makes him stand even above a Cleared Theta Clear who has full command power over the physical universe, yes, but cannot yet escape the necessity to be manifested in it.
The vibrations of a 7th-dynamic Clear would be so fine that only someone of comparable nature could perceive them. They are on the level of pure postulates. And as he stands outside any entanglement with mest he would be well dispositioned to create whole worlds by a mere postulate – which, naturally, is the reason for the existence of the mest universe.

A *Clear on the 8th dynamic* cannot possibly exist. This would be a contradiction in itself, because infinity is above action;

therefore infinity cannot make one react. On the 8th dynamic there is infinite ARC – or, reversely, no ARC at all. Which is, interestingly enough, the same. The reasoning behind this: ARC contains communication, and an important element of the communication formula is "distance". Distance again presupposes the existence of two terminals. However, when there are two thetans co-existing in infinity, there cannot be any distance between them. It takes a beingness to create distance and therewith duality; all of which is situated on the 7th dynamic. On the 8th dnamic there is no duality, no distance, no communication. Only co-existence in infinity (Ax. 25).

The crucial ability a Clear must have, by our definition, consists of duplicating and understanding anything he receives as an inflow. This would form the necessary prerequisite for gradually becoming an OT on the dynamic in question. Because: how would one be able to *act*, i.e outflow a communication, when there is no reality and affinity with the terminal one is aiming at – no matter whether one wishes to heal a plant, break down a wall or smooth out a quarrel. OT-ness means KRC and competence, it means getting the product no matter how. Whether by purely exterior means or by the brute force of sledgehammers – what counts is that the wall comes down in the end. The product tells the tale; all else is a matter of style and elegance.

In Hubbard's words: *"The supreme test of a thetan is his ability to make things go right"* [2]. On the first seven dynamics this means "no more" than fulfilling one's obligations in one's private life, towards one's family, in one's business, as a responsible member of the population of Earth, as a user of nature in its organic and inorganic aspects, and as a culturally, artistically and spiritually interested person. Within the framework of one's own goals, naturally, and with different priorities on each one, certainly – but still: in order to have all these aspects of life runing well under one's control and in an ethical manner, one has to be pretty OT.

Case Completion means: end of negative gain. After that would follow the "interest levels", where one would cultivate those abilities one is most interested in: positive gain. And should it be part of the life goal and purpose of someone that he learn to fully exteriorize – he will learn it, no doubt. (Hubbard's initial processes for this, by the way, are given in the books "Scientology 8-8008" and "Creation of Human Ability".)

One would have to approach the whole subject pragmatically, precisely in the spirit of the programme quoted already in Part One, where Hubbard says: *"If you think for a moment that it is the purpose of Scientology to produce something intensely spectacular like a ghost that can move cigarette paper or mountains, you have definitely gotten the wrong idea. We are interested in well men, we are interested in people with well bodies who think straight and who co-operate on optimum solutions. We are not making magicians. There are a great many things which a thetan or the analytical mind can do, but all these, until you are certain of them, belong in the field of para-Scientology and are only interesting data"* [12]. "Para-Scientology" is *"that large bin which includes all greater or lesser uncertainties"* [2].

SCIENTOLOGY AND MAGIC – A DIGRESSION

In the course of the last section, when we discussed possible Clear-abilites on dynamics 5, 6 and 7, we touched upon the border between scientology and magic – which is precisely the area of para-scientology. There you find the shadowy existence of phenomena about which the experienced and pragmatically oriented auditor has the "greater or lesser uncertainties" quoted above.

The reason he feels ill at ease about them is that quite a number of practical session problems – in particular with regard to the solo, or "advanced", levels – stem from such wishes of the public as cannot be satisfied within the scope of scientology. It's not that scientology was failing there – it's simply not on its line! There ought to be a clear statement about this at some point, so we take the opportunity now.

176

Some may be disappointed to hear that scientology – as mentioned in the previous section – "isn't as far as that yet". They may say: "These OTs don't even manage to knock tables about or read the future, which is as easy as child's play for any ordinary poltergeist or, respectively, any halfway decent medium. So why should one bother with it?" Well, wait a moment. When Hubbard talks about Theta Clear and Cleared Theta Clear, he is following other goals than those the adept of a magic circle would be envisioning. Many a frustrated "OT" would have been well advised to join a secret esoteric society instead of doing the solo-levels. This is because scientology and magic have two distinctly different aims, if not fundamentally different ethical principles. (Hubbard, who had intimate knowledge of the sex-magic of the then world-famous magician Aleister Crowley, was undoubtedly aware of this.)

Magic teaches "siddhis", as the Hindus call it, meaning the powers of the sorcerer. Amongst them you find healing by the touch of one's hand, instant healing, healing and killing over a distance, fire walking, runing spikes through one's tongue whilst in trance, reading the future e.g. in a crystal ball, conveying definite messages telepathically (e.g. for the secret services), astral walking, levitating and many other feats. These things can be learned. Esoteric knowledge has always been guarded by priests and been taught in temples since there were people on this planet; up to this day there are mystery schools in existence. In order to acquire these forms of OT-ness, one does not have to have crossed any scientological bridges or be Clear or OT in the sense of Hubbard.

Performances of this character nevertheless count as *the* criteria amongst some scientologists, to judge the "maturity" of an OT by. Someone who cannot levitate is no OT, and that's it on that! Much as such feats may appear to be criteria to certain people, they are in fact not. This is because of the above-mentioned difference between scientology and magic. In scientology one works towards *dissolving* ridges and entities of whatever kind. In magic however one strives to *create* new entities, and to command about and *use* already existing ones. Whether one is dealing with black or white magic is a matter of the underlying evil or, respectively, good intention; it is not a matter of the technique being used. Whoever can heal someone by prayers can just as well kill him the same way, no problem [23]. Consequently Scientology cannot be compared to white or black magic. The task of the auditor consists of rehabilitating the self-determinism of a being and of eliminating the aberrating influences of mental masses and energies on the thetan. In order to achieve this, the auditor does not send the annoying masses, ridges and entities back to their creator with the intention to destroy him by means of the destruction postulates contained in the attacking entity (a possible defense in the case of death prayers), no, he dissolves, erases, as-ises them. Their effect, no matter when it was calculated to come off, is thereby cancelled.

The auditor is pan-determined and impartial. He does not restore peace by throwing the bomb back where it came from, but by discharging all ammunition and drawing it out of circulation. He audits games conditions below 2.0 on the tone scale, the kind characterized by the hardened self-determinism called "eye for an eye, tooth for a tooth"; he wishes to create positive games conditions in the form of optimum solutions, ideally even pan-determined no-games conditions. Scientology therefore addresses itself to the dissolving of unwanted conditions; black magic, in contrast, to the solidification, the clustering of black masses and their employment in the control of beings; white magic concentrates on the use of entities in order to achieve good effects.

The aim of scientology, in a word, is: "More ethics!" Optimum solutions on as many dynamics as possible; in particular on the higher ones. Pre-Clear and solo auditor both strive to create order and conditions worth living in, be it privately, within the framework of society, or on the subtle level of entities and theta-quanta. "More ethics!" is the motto, not the mastering of spiritual circus tricks, not the accumulation of personal power by magical mystery forces. Scientology is an attempt to advance towards a fundamental understanding of existence, and responsibility for it, as opposed to development of power merely to manipulate what already exists. There *is* the possibility of evil. Instead of using it or fighting it, one ought to grow above it.

How, under these circumstances, could one as a scientologist possibly demonstrate one's OT-ness? One would rather excel through the absence of such tricks! In the case of mental attacks one would show untouchability and lack of aggressiveness; one would put the blame on the correct source – more likely than not even on oneself. One would stay unnoticed. A maxim could be tailored from this: the more someone controls his life and the less attention he draws, the bigger and wider he plays and the more innocuous he stays, the more he is OT. This thought places scientology in direct line with Buddhism and Taoism. There, the chief characteristic of the sage is that he does *not* leave any traces.

Someone might object that Hubbard is propagating precisely the thing condemned above, when he talks of Theta Clear and Cleared Theta Clear. Yes and no. The emphasis is not quite in the same place. It is quite up to the OT to decide if he works white or black magic, i.e. creates theta-quanta and sends them about for his own use. Whoever wishes to create effects on a spiritual level in the manner of magicians cannot but work with theta-quanta. However, an OT – if he were to follow the tenets of scientology ethics – would dissolve them all after use! This is of paramount importance in this context. This makes the difference. And below it all there is his continuous intention to disentangle each and every circumstance not in keeping with an optimum solution.

Which takes us back to the subject of postulates: whose postulates created the unwanted circumstances? Working on it from this angle means all by itself that one would contribute to the senior product of an ethical order. That one would approach the area of "superhuman feats" in the process would certainly be a nice side product worth following up – but it would never stand in the focus of one's purposes.

As a summary we might say that a person intent on the attainment of magical effects should attend the pertinent schools, because scientology, being merely interested in the increase of ethics, could be a disappointment for him. Nevertheless, it would not be a bad thing at all if Clears and OTs consulted precisely these schools of magic on order to enhance their general spiritual education! Partly because such knowledge has been used powerfully in the past to entrap and cause harm, partly because, in order to achieve an ethical order, one has to have a full working knowledge of what dangers exist. To reduce the field of para-scientology in size by increased research and inter-disciplinary comparison, is yet another task for the future. (And quite in keeping with the "Code of Scientologist" [1].)

THE BRIDGE IN PRACTICE

The crossing of the auditing bridge is done in three stages: the first from beginning to Clear, the second from Clear to Case Completion, the third after Case Completion. Let us look at them one after the other.

First stage: Up to Clear home-made ridges from one's own track are usually handled; the occasional entity may slip in here and there. The pc soon recognizes which are his and which aren't and learns to tell them apart. From Clear on he keeps himself clean by making sure not to create new ridges or get tied up with foreign ones. Should he do this he is usually able to dissolve them immediately, even without the use of an E-meter.

Taking it step by step, the sequence is roughly like this: To start with, one would audit what the pc is most troubled with and therefore most interested in. He will tell the auditor all about it in his *Introductory Interview.* The auditor analyzes the case, selects the most suitable processes and audits a **Life Repair**. A Life Repair may concern the pc's social situation, in which case his rudiments on life will be "put in". It may concern psychosomatic illnesses, in which case engrams, GPMs and postulates are found and audited.

The end phenomenon (EP) of a Life Repair occurs when the pc feels happy about his present life and when his complaints have disappeared. This result would be the absolute optimum. More usually, though, the mere fact of having discharged his trouble spots does not change the pc's life circumstances immediately. But he can confront them now, go out, roll up his sleeves and do something about them.

Look at the reality of it: the pc has had 25 or 40 hours of Life Repair within two or three weeks. He has discharged all his worries regarding his family and his company and knows the reason for them. As well he has found the engram which keeps his hip from healing. Up to this point, all these changes have happened in his first universe only. His family and the company (third universe) haven't been affected by his positive changes yet. So he has to go out and DO IT in the third universe. He has to make his new positiveness *happen* out there. A little study program on the subjects of ethics and management will assist him in this phase, provide guidelines and increase his KRC on life. (Auditing has increased the *ARC*. But that's not all it takes, as we have seen.) And regarding his hip, he has to actually *take* vitamins and minerals and exercises to make it heal properly. The engram is gone, yes, and now healing can occur where before it couldn't. But he still has to actively look after his leg (KRC) to make it heal all the way.

During the auditing it may happen that the pc has big cognitions on his postulates and on himself being the cause for all his troubles. He may realize that it is himself who keeps the case there. Which is to say that the pc may go Clear as the EP of the Life Repair.

If he doesn't, he will come back after he has settled in on his new level of ARC/KRC in life, and want some more auditing. Why? Because he has *expanded*. He has grown, hit new walls, overcome them, hit some more walls, got a bloody nose, and now wonders why. Again he gets an interview, and again suitable processes are selected. He may get an **Expanded Life**

181

Repair now, again in the style of rudiment running or engram handling, depending. Or he may get a number of processes called the **Grades**. The "Scientology Grades" are five sets of processes, each dealing with a separate subject. Grade 0: communication. Grade I: problems. Grade II: overts/withholds. Grade III: life ruins. Grade IV: service facsimiles. There are as well the less frequently needed Grades V to VII.

With this done, the pc will eventually go Clear. Nobody will tell him so, by the way. Because of his general technical knowledge he will come up with this realization himself and inform the auditor. Now an auditing action called the ***Clear Check*** ensues; it confirms the state or demonstrates that the pc is not Clear yet and should get some more auditing.

Up to this point, he has handled home-made charge. It may have happened that a foreign-made ridge slipped in during one session or the other, but as long as the pc took it as his own it will have gone by unnoticed. However, as the pc approaches Clear, his level of differentiation will increase and he won't "buy it" anymore when a foreign-made incident pops up in session. The session will stall unless the auditor helps the pc to identify the correct source of the ridge. It may well happen that the pc goes over more and more into handling foreign-made ridges, simply because there are none of his own left. This means that he has gone Clear because his ARC (tonelevel and confront) has increased so much that his own ridges have dissolved and vanished. Yet his KRC remains wanting: he can spot the composite case as the source of trouble (which is the mark of a Clear) but he cannot handle it yet.

To do so, he studies to become a solo auditor and audits his **Solo Assists**. He audits processes which stabilize him and keep the composite case off his back. He undoes everything which may have connected up with him. The purpose of the Solo Assists is the disconnection from foreign entities in order to keep one's space clean and free.

Second stage: How come that the thetan should have this mass of foreign-made ridges and entities stuck to him at all? Quite simple: He went in contact with them because he was sufficiently aware of them to recognize their existence, but he was not willing to confront or able to as-is them. At the moment of making contact with them, he counter-created against them in an effort to make them disappear from his awareness (not-is). Thereby he contributed to the already existing ridge by adding his own theta energy quanta to it. Thus a lasting connection was formed. As a consequence the ridge is even harder to as-is since the number of its creators (thetans) who contributed to it with their theta-quanta, has increased by one more. Therefore the authorship of each quantum is that much harder to identify and the as-ising, which only comes about by correct designation of authorship, is harder to do. The more creators (authors) a ridge has, the harder it is to take it apart. (Dn Ax. 118; Ax. 32, 34.)

Example: Fred takes a walk through the forest. He passes a spot – without knowing about it – where they used to hang people from the gallows, some hundreds of years ago. All sorts of ridges and pictures from those days are still around. They stem from people who disagreed with getting hanged because it went against their survival postulates. So they considered it a stop, formed a succumb postulate and thus made a ridge. It is interesting to note that these ridges stay in their place no matter how much time may have passed and no matter where the thetan who made them happens to be. This is the reason for the spooks one can observe in some places.

Right there Fred sits down to take a rest. He gets an eerie feeling. As he looks at a strong bough, he reckons it would serve well for hanging someone and wonders about his own thought; he gets a tight sensation around the neck and throat; he gets pictures of dangling feet. Although he hasn't paid too much attention to any of this he nevertheless has communicated to one or more of these ridges by the act of perceiving them. He has gone into ARC with them. Technically, he has received a lock; except that the engram restimulated wasn't made on his track. It was a foreign-made one.

(The expression "going into ARC" doesn't mean that he thought these were pretty pictures. ARC is a flexible phenomenon occurring on a scale between +40 and −40. True, there is a survival/non-survival watershed at 2.0 on this scale (antagonism), but nonetheless it's ARC all the way from top to bottom, be it in its positive or its inverted form. – See Ax.25.)

Once the Clear has finished his Solo Assists, he goes one step further and actually picks out the entities of the composite case one after the other and audits *them*. The same rules as in any other auditing as well as the auditor's code apply. He audits them the same way and pretty much on the same processes he was audited on himself. It is a two-phase program: first he works on those entities he can perceive naturally, until none are left. Then an additional restimulation is necessary to "break some more bank loose" and make it available for auditing. The **OT III** materials serve this purpose.

In order to understand the full mechanism of this part of the bank the solo-auditor studies the OT III techniques and audits what he can find that way. When he runs out of entities, or meets situations he cannot resolve with OT III, the techniques of *Excalibur* will help him. They aim at a level of subtlety way beyond the scope of OT III techniques. By this action the solo auditor becomes engaged in resolving the "Earth case", i.e. the ridges left flying around due to Xenu's galactic power coup 75 million years ago, and due to other implants as well.

The end phenomenon of Excalibur is: foreign-made ridges gone, no more composite case. The solo auditor is now a free thetan with nothing to block his view outwards and with no masses to inhibit telepathic communications flowing towards him.

At this stage he will notice – much to his amazement – that there are games still going on he once (eons ago) was part of, that there are players still around he once was a team-mate of. (Remember: thetans do not die, and not all of them have bodies.) He discovers that there are quite some withholds and overts which were never cleaned up because the composite case interfered with the rather subtle communication lines from those former and present co-players and opponents. So he sits down and audits this level of *Games and Players*.

He is, by the way, dealing with home-made charge again. After all it was him who caused the incomplete cycles which made these players have attention on him since those bygone times. Towards the end of this level, he is however not dealing any more with "old" ridges, but finds himself involved in a telepathic struggle on the level of postulates, occurring in present time. Postulates one cannot register with an E-meter as they have no mass or energy, no mental mest. Postulates one can know, yet one cannot measure them. (For this reason the E-meter becomes increasingly unnecessary at this point.) Should one make the mistake, though, of resisting inflowing postulates (alter-is, not-is), *new* ridges will be created instantly – and for *their* erasure the E-meter may certainly be useful. Particularly when one has allowed it to go a bit too far.

Third stage: This is how far the bridge goes currently. As its result the thetan does not find himself engaged any more in games conditions with the composite case formed by Xenu or other political implant games of then or now. He has become a "single being" in the true sense of the word. He has come to the end of "negative gain" and can now develop his abilities in order to have positive gains. He can expand his OT-ness to his heart's desire without being encumbered by a reactive bank.

A Case Completion is neither an "automatic" nor an "absolute" state. It grows or decays depending on the thetan's awareness about higher dynamics and his willingnes to behave himself ethically and in accordance with ARC and KRC. A thetan has absolutely no problem creating another bank for himself. In the paragraph about "Games and Players" above you have seen how easy it is. You may think now: "But that's crazy! Nobody is going to make a bank for himself!" But oh yes, they do. And they even have the right to do so. (And remember: We have all started that way. Else we wouldn't be here.)

MORE THAN ONE BRIDGE

The sequence of steps from Life Repair to Case Completion given in this chapter represent one possible way of working. They do not correspond to what is sold in the CofS under the name of "The Bridge" (Trademark). *Their* "Bridge" looks different. Below Clear there are three blocks of auditing: Introductory – the Grades – Dianetics ("New Era Dianetics"). They have to be done by everybody, like it or not. Then follows a Clear attest which usually lacks any instruction as to why Clear was attested and what it actually means. Then the levels "New OT I to VII" are done, just as inescapably as the steps before Clear. This – as everybody is to suffer the same treatment standardly – the CofS considers "standard tech".

One cannot pretend, unfortunately, that things look much better outside the CofS – probably because most auditors working outside the CofS were trained *in* the CofS. Since free scientology splintered off the church in 1983, there came into being as many bridges as there are scientological sects. They are based – just as the one suggested here – on the degree of comprehension or miscomprehension the individual "bridge builder" has of Hubbard's work. A little hint to the potential bridge-crosser so that his doubts about the right choice may be dispelled: Just ask for the goal and purpose of the bridge in question. What does the other shore look like? When you only get to see glittering eyes and feel beaten down by stormy assertions instead of receiving a clear answer, I would – if I were in your place – withdraw politely.

BEYOND ALL BRIDGES

As we know from the Factors: *"Before the beginning there was a Cause and the entire purpose of the Cause was the creation of an effect"* (Fac. 1). So there was oneself, the non-postulating one. With a first postulate he created his own begining: *"In the beginning and forever there is the decision and the decision is TO BE"*

(Fac. 2). *Before* the beginning one existed as a potential, *in* the beginning one exists in actuality. With Factor 2 the game has started. Precisely there is our often-quoted 1st postulate.

What is there above Factor 1 then, above oneself as cause? A difficult question and hard to answer, because as soon as one sets out to find an answer one finds oneself being cause! For this reason it says in Factor 30: *"And above these things there might be speculation only."* So let us go ahead and speculate – if not above the Factors, so at least along their upper edge, within the bracket of Factors 1–4.

If one took the concept of the 1st postulate to its extreme, one might say that the whole reason for the existence of a thetan in his non-static state, that of a player, depended on one single postulate, made eons ago, with which he started his game cycles. It is this postulate by which he lowered himself from a hypothetical state of "pure static" to the level of a player and became involved with the dynamics.

"The ultimate truth is a static" (Ax. 35). This is one of the two important data here. You, the reader, are static (or eternal, if you wish) to the extent that you have recognized yourself as the ultimate truth. The other important datum is taken from the Know-To-Mystery Scale: a postulate implies a not-know. Therefore a postulate (no matter what postulate) always is a lie with reference to the ultimate truth, insofar as the ultimate truth implies knowing all, whereas postulating implies not knowing all (Ax. 25, 37). You, as the ultimate truth, pretend to not-know, thereby lie to yourself – and stop being the ultimate truth (Ax. 44-46). To say "I know that I not-know" does not help much as it does not contain the answer to *what* it is that you not-know.

In order to have a game, the ultimate truth *must* lie to himself. To play a game, to enter the field of dynamics, there must be barriers. Without barriers there is no game. Not-knowing of course is a barrier; knowing all, on the other hand, is a no-game condition. Considering to not-know something and then going to find out about it, is the start of any game.

If there were a thetan with only one single postulate and without any alter-is of it, there would be nothing left on him to be restimulated. No case. There would only be action towards the postulated purpose (Dn Ax. 190). His game would be over as soon as this single postulate were fulfilled, i.e. executed in reality, or cancelled by the thetan himself. At this moment the existence of this thetan would be without goal and purpose. His beingness, his reason for existence would be redeemed. There would be no game any more, therefore no purposes/barriers/freedoms, therefore an infinite potential of purposes/barriers/freedoms, therefore infinite beingness, infinite doingness, infinite havingness – and that is static. (Please note that beingness, doingness and havingness denote *states*, not actions.)

At this point the thetan would vanish as a player and become a "pure static". He would be infinite, he would *be* the 8th dynamic. You could not locate him anywhere as he has *"no mass, no motion, no wavelength, no location in space or time"*. Yet he always has *"the ability to postulate and perceive"* (Ax. 1). Having an ability does not necessarily mean that one must use it all the time. He doesn't *have* to postulate and perceive – unless he wishes to start another game. He may as well stay in this state of "pure static".

How long would one remain in this state? How long were you static the last time you had this state? –These questions cannot be answered; they are self-contradictory and put the wrong way. Firstly the concept of static excludes the concept of time. Therefore one cannot possiby ask: "How long were you static the last time?" Time is brought about through the cycle of action. As a full static does not act at all but simply *knows*, there is no time to that state. Secondly, a state of "pure static" is merely hypothetical. In practice the thetan has a dual quality: that of player in the game and that of static above the games (Ax. 1, 48; Dn Ax. 1–5). This double quality can be experienced. If one did not have an inkling of it, one would not wish to go up the bridge to Case Completion, finish one's game and become a "pure static" once again. One feels one is "down here" and wants to get back "up there".

Now, what "part of him" got stuck in the mest universe? – Well, of course that part which is identified with a beingness and introverted into a viewpoint (Fac. 24; Ax. 45, 46).

This, then, is the message of the Axioms and Factors: the thetan as player and the thetan as static co-exist perpetually. One is static "all the time", simply because time does not exist. As well and along with static, one is actively playing. This results in the ideal game situation for a thetan: that of "action", tone 20 on the emotional tone scale. Here one is fully aware of both one's static-ness and one's senior games postulate. No alter-is has been put up against it yet. He plays "full blast"; his intention knows no reservation. Yet one does not feel a "lone ranger" but embedded in a flowing web of postulates which one aligns oneself with and which one in turn influences. One feels included in a whole universe of games going on concurrently. Therefore anybody's action determinates one's own and vice versa. *"All thought is concerned with motion"* (Dn Ax. 23).

What could one possibly do wrong at this level of lusty immortality? Are there any ethical standards at all? You cannot kill a thetan, therefore anything is permitted, one might think. But no. Even here there are agreements with regard to an optimum solution, guaranteeing the continuation of "The Game". They are expressed in the two "Rights of a Thetan" Hubbard formulated in 1952 on the Philadelphia Doctorate Course. They are the "Right To One's Self-Determinism" and the "Right To Leave A Game". To leave one is always more difficult than to start one, as we have seen. Which is mainly one's own fault as the counter-postulates stem from oneself and no-one else. Yet apart from that one may get stopped from leaving a game by implants – which is only possible by the implanter using the self-created masses already there, in order to stick his own to them and thereby pull one even deeper into mest. The possible argument in defense of implanting, "His own fault – shouldn't have made any masses to start with!", has no validity. The point to be observed is that implanting is not a "games accident" but a deliberate suppresion. Seen in this light, the two

Rights represent the highest possible ethical standard. Implanting is the heaviest possible offense against them.

At tone 20 on the tone scale the two Rights are made the most of. Here the thetan plays his game self-determinedly (1st Right) and with the certainty of being free to leave it any time (2nd Right). He has not yet created anything which might keep him against his will – and therefore no-one else could.

Faites votre jeux!

Bibliography

(1) "Scn 0-8", by L. Ron Hubbard (LRH), 1970.
(2) "Technical Dictionary", by LRH, 1975.
(3) "Dianetics, Modern Science of Mental Health", by LRH, 1950, edition of 1973.
(4) "The Sad Tale of Scientology", by Eric Tonwnsend, 1985.
(5) "History of Man", by LRH, 1952.
(6) "The Phoenix Lectures", by LRH, 1954.
(7) "The Hidden Story of Scientology", by Omar Garrison, 1974.
(8) "Operation Mind Control", by Walter Bowart, 1978.
(9) "Playing Dirty", by Omar Garrison, 1980.
(10) "The Secret World of Interpol", Omar V. Garrison, London 1977.
(11) "Keeping Scientology Working", HCO PL 7 Feb 1965.
(12) "Professional Auditor's Bulletin" Nr.2., Technical Bulletins, Volume I, 1976.
(13) "Creation of Human Ability", by LRH, 1954.
(14) "Tech Bulletins", Vol. I.
(15) "Fundamentals of Thought", by LRH, 1956.
(16) "Science of Survival", by LRH, 1951.
(17) "The Volunteer Minister's Handbook", by LRH, 1976.
(18) "How to choose your people", by Ruth Minshull, 1973.
(19) "Modern Management Technology Defined", By LRH, 1976.
(20) "Tech Bulletins", Vol. II.
(21) "The Way Of The White Clouds", by Lama Govinda, 1966.
(22) "Autobiography of a Yogi", by Yogananda, 1946.
(23) "The secret science behind miracles", by Max F. Long, Huna Research Publications, Vista/California.

HCO PL of 25 June AD 13 (1963)

HCO P/L of 25 June AD 13

Scientologists Only

CONFIDENTIAL

An International Objective
(This Pol Lt is ~~Confidential~~
for Scientologists and
The attacked plan is however ~~not~~
BPI ~~Confidential~~. When
republishing the attacked
plan to the public or Scientology magazines
do not publish
this covering policy
letter.)

When we were attacked
in January for using E-

meters, I ~~applied~~
~~research~~ adopted for
A 2 part policy:

(1) To hold the line
legally and win in
courts where possible
but in no event to
lose ground;

(2) To speed up
research, by passing
clear and then clear
as objectives, abandon
work on the technology that go
interim states and

concentrating on the
attainment by auditing
of the state of O.T.
as the best forward answer
to our difficulties.

In part one of
this programme, we are
succeeding easily. But
it is only short term
and world deterioration
is accelerating.

In part two we
have achieved the

technology necessary
by an incredible speed
up and gain. We now
have O.T. in direct
and real sight with
only a few hundred hours
of actual auditing
intervening. VENING This is
astonishing break
through, a real big
boot-straps necessity
level research spru
We are then al

months away from having O.T.s, a year at the most.

No scientologist need be told what that means.

This fact enters us upon forward planning. The trouble with O.T.s in the past has only been lack of cooperation and a commonly agreed upon objective survive. The proof is, O.T.s have not survived as O.T.s Whenever this super-individuation collided with the super organization of weaker beings. The answer is to remain organized, with mutual assistance and integrity and not lose touch with or responsibility for all

Without these O.T.s eventually fell prey again to smaller beings with bigger organization skill, O.T. is an unstable state only when O.T.s are not cooperating with O.T.s but each one going his own way in the strong but fatious belief he can single-handedly

levels of life forms and societies.

This means that programmes for such agreement must be offered.

The first step is to prevent atomic war and planetary chaos and to utilize Earth as a rehabilitation centre since it has already had the

Technology established here. A second step following after would be to establish units not unlike central organizations, in nearby systems.

The real conflict will ~~follow~~ stellar powers interested in these areas will develop as I can vouch for the two most concerned in this galaxy, the Espinal United Stars and the to which the Solar System distantly belongs and the Galactic Confederation to which Espinal moderately bows.

As not all living things are capable of attaining O.T. (the vast bulk of a population (are ~~possibly~~ minion in origin) the task of rehabilitation is not as great as it looks.

This leaves us first and foremost with the problem faced by the budding O.T. What to do to square things around?

I recommend that any action taken by any O.T. on this planet be guided by the attached programme "On International Objective". Any public ambitions for us on Earth, any vengeful or destructive urges, any stunts or public actions should be channeled into accomplishing the attached programme

Several OT.s even if acting independently could accomplish this, even making errors Further the plan has some chance of succeeding even if driven in ordinary ways such as placing copies of it in the various offices of the United Nations putting it into newspaper inviting the attention of large commercial interests to it, etc

We could probably each one of us think of a plan for Earth let us instead agree upon a feasible plan in which all of us can cooperate.

ANY PRECLEAR MOVING TOWARD O.T. SHOULD READ THIS POLICY LETTER AND THE PLAN. THE PUBLIC MAY BE SHOWN THIS PLAN AND IT MAY BE REPUBLISHED ANYWHERE. THIS POLICY LETTER HOWEVER MAY NOT BE MADE PUBLIC.

Index

SCIENTOLOGY

– A Handbook For Use

The Procedures.

•

•   •

Professional Application.

EDITION SCIENTERRA

ISBN 3-922367-27-5   Verkehrs-Nr.: 16 645